Commerce and Business

Commerce and Business

Derek Thomas, MA, BSc (Econ), PhD has wide experience as teacher, chief examiner and moderator. He is an author whose simple, straightforward approach to the teaching of commercial subjects has been enthusiastically received by teachers and pupils.

Commerce and Business

Derek Thomas

Chambers Commerce Series

Published by W & R Chambers Ltd Edinburgh, 1989

British Library Cataloguing in Publication Data
Thomas, Derek
  Commerce and business
  1. Commerce   2. Business studies
  I. Title
  380.1

ISBN 0-550-20712-0

Acknowledgement
The author wishes to thank Miss M S Lawrence who typed the original manuscript.

Typeset by Bookworm Typesetting Ltd, Edinburgh

Printed in Great Britain by
Richard Clay Ltd, Bungay, Suffolk

Contents

Chapter 4 Retailers and Suppliers

Chapter 5 Wholesale Trade

Chapter 6 Markets

Chapter 7 Consumers

Chapter 8 Private Enterprise

Chapter 9 Public Ownership

Chapter 10 Stock Exchanges

Chapter 11 The Results of Trading

Chapter 12 Exports and Imports

PART II THE AIDS TO TRADE

Chapter 13 Banks

Preface

The aim of this volume is to provide a textbook on Commerce suitable for students preparing for General Certificate of Secondary Education examinations. It is designed also for students taking the Commerce examinations of the London Chamber of Commerce Examinations Board, Pitman Examinations Institute, University of Cambridge Local Examinations Syndicate (overseas candidates) and the University of London School Examinations Board (overseas candidates). It also provides a useful text for candidates taking RSA Background to Business examinations. Those studying GCE Advanced Level Economics and other economics courses for examinations set by the professional bodies will find the book to be valuable background reading. People engaged in commercial occupations, whether in trade or in one of the services ancillary to trade, will find the book to be useful in identifying how particular occupations fit into the general scheme of commerce.

At the end of each chapter there is a Test Yourself exercise designed to assist with understanding the text.

D.T.

PART I
HOME AND FOREIGN TRADE

Chapter 1

The Meaning of Commerce

1.1 Why Do People Go To Work?

Many people spend a considerable part of their waking hours at work. The factory worker controls machines. The miner extracts mineral deposits from the earth. The clerk records business transactions. The dentist treats patients. Transport workers move people and goods from place to place by land, sea or air.

Why does all this activity take place? People who work would say that they do so in order to earn wages or a salary. But money is not wanted for its own sake; it is wanted for what it will buy. Money is wanted for the purpose of satisfying wants.

There are three main things which are wanted by everyone. They are:

- food and drink
- clothing
- shelter.

After people have sufficient food, clothing and house-room, they try to satisfy their other wants. For instance, some may want motor-cycles or cars; others may prefer better houses. If people were asked to write out lists of the things they wanted, the lists would reveal a wide variety of desires.

If people had no wants or if wants could be satisfied without any effort there would be no need to work. People work so that they may consume. They are *consumers*, that is, they buy goods with the money they earn.

Money is essential, therefore, to satisfy wants – and a person's standard of living is determined by the amount of goods that he or she may consume.

1.2   Production

People who go to work are producers as well as being consumers. A miner produces coal, an insurance agent sells insurance and a solicitor sells skill in handling legal matters. In fact, everyone who goes to work is helping to produce *goods* or, as in the case of the solicitor and the insurance agent, to provide *services*.

Production means the provision of goods and the provision of services, the aim of which is to satisfy people's wants.

The organisation of production

Most people earn their living by doing one particular job only. A person is an accountant, or a carpenter, or a welder, and he or she specialises in that particular occupation. Workers are specialists because industry is organised on the basis of the division of labour – that is, the production of an article is divided into a larger number of different operations. Thus, in the making of a pair of shoes nearly one hundred distinct operations take place. Workers are employed to perform one particular operation and they become specialists. A visit to a factory will help the reader to understand the system. As the product moves slowly along the assembly line each worker performs a particular task. When the product reaches the end of the line, it is ready for dispatch to customers.

Historically, the system of division of labour began in the dividing up of the day's work among the members of the family. With the growth of towns, this extended to the specialisation of individual trades, and with the development of the factory system it came to mean the division of work into a number of processes, each being performed by a different worker. The development of foreign trade has enabled countries to specialise in producing certain commodities, so that division of labour has been established on an international scale.

The system of the division of labour has certain advantages and limitations.

Advantages of the division of labour
The first advantage of specialisation is increased production. In the early days of the car industry one worker built an entire engine. Henry Ford split the work into 84 operations, each of which was performed by a different person. The result was that

the output of 84 workers was trebled. When workers are specialists, repetition of the same operation increases speed and skill and more goods are produced.

A second advantage is that various abilities can be used to the full. It is far more beneficial for everyone when a brain surgeon can spend time in the operating theatre rather than having to give part of the day to the making of clothes to wear or the repair of a faulty car. It follows also that the simplification of tasks resulting from specialisation means that firms are able to find a proportion of suitable jobs for disabled persons.

Thirdly, when a process is broken down into a series of specialised and simplified tasks, a job takes a shorter time to learn, and workers feel less reluctant to train for a new job.

From an employer's point of view, the specialisation of processes means that output can be measured very accurately. If the assembly line is moving at a given speed then so many products will be coming off the line every hour. Thus a day's or month's or year's output can be estimated fairly accurately.

Finally, no time is lost between the performance of the various processes, as might well be the case if one person was responsible for making the complete product.

Disadvantages of the division of labour
Whilst production based on the specialisation of jobs has certain benefits, its adoption has resulted, nevertheless, in certain drawbacks.

1 A worker who performs the same task for a number of hours each day is, sooner or later, going to find that the work is monotonous. Firms have tried to combat boredom in various ways, ranging from the provision of 'piped' music to the granting of a rest period during a part of every hour, but the problem remains.

   On the other hand, the greater output of goods and services resulting from the specialisation of jobs has raised the standard of living and enabled workers to enjoy far more leisure than was once the case. As production is further expanded, the working week is likely to get even shorter and, probably, annual holidays will be longer.

2 The goods produced under a system of specialisation are usually standardised products. This is evident in the design of cars, domestic appliances, and houses. Whether or not standardisation is a disadvantage is really a matter of opinion.

After all, consumers can pay extra for houses or cars built to their particular requirements.

3 A more important disadvantage is that instability of employment may result from the application of the division of labour. Workers in one industry are very often dependent on those before them in the process of production. Thus a prolonged stoppage in the coal or steel industries may throw thousands of other workers out of work because supplies of these raw materials stop. The same is true within an industry. Interdependence in car manufacture is such that the decision of a handful of workers to strike can put thousands of other workers out of work within hours.

1.3   Barter and Money

The ultimate object of going to work is to acquire useful things in exchange for that work. Employees are not paid in the form of directly useful things, but in the form of money. Greengrocers do not resort to barter (the exchange of goods for goods.) They do not supply their customers with fruit and vegetables in exchange for bread, clothes, newspapers and other requirements. A greengrocer's produce is sold for money which is spent upon the things the greengrocer wishes to buy. This arrangement is convenient for everyone concerned.

A baker who supplied the greengrocer with bread and had to take payment in lettuces and carrots, might either dislike these foodstuffs or have sufficient stocks of them already. Consequently the produce would have to be re-sold, which takes time and might be very inconvenient. To replace these complicated sales by the use of money saves a great deal of trouble. A baker who takes payment in money is free to spend it on whatever is wanted and does not need to accept goods in payment which may or may not be wanted.

Thus the use of money as a medium of exchange overcomes the drawbacks of the barter system.

1.4   Kinds of Occupations

People who earn a living follow occupations which can be classified in the following way:

Fig. 1.1 *Kinds of occupations*

Industry

Industrial workers obtain raw materials such as coal or clay and change them into finished products.
There are three main types of industry, namely:

(i)   extractive or primary
(ii)   manufacturing or secondary
(iii) constructive or tertiary.

People who work in *extractive* industries are employed to obtain raw materials from the land or sea. Some examples of extractive industries are:

- agriculture, that is, the growing of foodstuffs and raw materials, and the rearing of cattle and sheep;
- mining and quarrying, that is, extracting coal, iron ore, salt, china-clay, slate, sand, limestone and other important minerals from the earth;
- fishing;
- forestry, that is, the cultivation of forests to provide a supply of timber;
- drilling for oil.

People who work in the *manufacturing* industries use the raw materials obtained by workers in the extractive industries and change them into finished products. For example, raw cotton may be converted into dress material; clay may be fashioned into cups and saucers; wood may be made into furniture.
People who work in *constructive* industries assemble finished products made in manufacturing into different forms. For example, bricks, tiles, door frames, window frames, glass and other manufactured products are assembled by the building industry to form houses, shops, warehouses and factories. In the motor car industry, tyres, sparking plugs, car bodies and hundreds of other component parts are fitted together to make

vehicles. Other constructive industries include road-making and the laying of railway tracks.

Commerce

People who work in commercial occupations are engaged in assisting the movement of raw materials in industry and the distribution of finished goods from industry to consumers. Commerce is concerned, therefore, with the buying and selling of goods at any stage in their progress from raw materials to finished goods. In addition, commerce covers the various services provided to finance, store, insure, transport and publicise goods during production. The divisions of commerce are shown in figure 1.2.

Fig. 1.2   *Divisions of commerce*

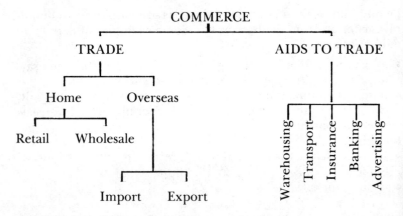

Trade
Trade means buying and selling in either home or foreign markets. Thus people who work in the import and export trades are commercial workers. The wholesale and retail trades link up manufacturers turning out goods in large quantities and consumers who buy only small amounts at a time.

Warehousing
Warehouses provide storage facilities for goods until they are required. Many goods have a seasonal demand. For example,

summer clothes made during the winter months must be stored until consumers wish to buy them; Christmas trade goods are made early in the year and must be stored until needed.

Transport
Transport by road, rail, sea and air distributes raw materials and finished goods to where they are required at home or abroad.

Insurance
Insurance provides compensation for damage to, or loss of, goods and raw materials. Hence traders are relieved of some of the risks to which goods (both in the course of transport and in store) are liable.

Banking
Banks assist traders by providing:

- the cheque system and other means of payment of goods;
- financial assistance in the form of bank loans.

Advertising
Advertising provides consumers with information about goods available for sale and seeks to promote sales by persuading people to try them or to buy more.

Warehousing, transport, insurance, banking, and advertising are sometimes called the aids to trade because they help to make buying and selling safer and simpler.

Direct services

Some people are employed neither in industry or commerce, that is they do not help to produce or distribute goods. Instead they contribute services of various kinds directly to people. Some examples of direct service workers are:

- civil servants and local government officials employed in administering a wide range of public services, such as education, public health and housing;
- police and fire services, protecting life and property;
- members of the armed forces who contribute to the defence of the country;

- professional sportspeople, actors, musicians and other entertainers who help people to relax and enjoy their leisure time;
- doctors, dentists, opticians, nurses, pharmacists and others who provide medical care;
- teachers in schools and colleges, library staff and laboratory technicians who contribute to the education service;
- hairdressers, solicitors, window-cleaners, decorators and many others who offer a wide range of personal services.

Direct services are important because they contribute to the efficiency of people during their working hours. For example, medical care keeps people fit; various personal services (such as window-cleaning and decorating) save people time so that they can devote themselves more fully to their own jobs; entertainers contribute to the enjoyment of leisure so that people may return refreshed to their work.

Test Yourself

1 Why do people go to work?
2' Write down a person's three basic wants.
3 What is a consumer?
4 What do you understand by the phrase 'standard of living'?
5 Write down the meaning of 'production'.
6 How would you describe a system of producing goods in which the work is broken down into a number of different operations?
7 What is the meaning of 'barter'?
8 Write down two disadvantages of barter.
9 List the three main groups of occupations.
10 Give two types of industry and two examples of each type.
11 What is the meaning of 'commerce'?
12 What does 'trade' mean?
13 Write down the 'aids to trade'.
14 What is the meaning of direct service occupations?
15 Classify the following occupations: bank clerk, oil-well driller, jockey, pop musician, fishmonger, member of parliament, accountant, tobacconist, army officer.

Chapter 2

Retailing Through Shops

Shops take a variety of forms. The main differences lie in what the shops sell and in their size. One sells clothes, while another sells groceries. One is a large store employing scores of assistants and selling many types of goods, while another is owned by one person and offers a particular group of products.

2.1 Retail Functions and Services

All shops seek to offer certain basic services.

1 A shop provides the goods that customers want. The retailer (shopkeeper) studies the needs and tastes of customers and assembles a selection of merchandise to meet those requirements. If the exact item required is not available, a customer will be dissatisfied and may well go elsewhere. The retailer therefore has to keep many lines in stock and try never to run out of any of them. As well as stocking a variety of products, the retailer stocks different makes of the same type of goods to allow customers as wide a choice as possible.

2 A shop provides goods at the time when customers want them. The retailer opens the shop for most of the day and waits for customers to come to buy when it suits them. The retailer may open early in the morning for the convenience of early morning shift workers, and stay open late in the evening in order to attract the custom of those who have been at work during the day.

3 A shop provides goods that are suitable in quantity to customers' requirements. The word 'retail' means to cut up or cut off, and the breaking down of large quantities into single items is the prime service given by the retailer. Cases of goods ('wholes') are bought from the wholesaler and split into sizes that will suit the customer. At one time, the retailer weighed,

measured and packed goods but a great deal of this work is done nowadays by the manufacturer.

In addition to the three major functions outlined above, a retailer may provide any or all of the following services for customers:

- delivery of goods;
- the collection of orders by calling at the homes of customers;
- the ordering of goods not in stock;
- advice on purchases: a retailer is the specialist who can help the shopper to judge the value, quality and performance of an article. In addition, a retailer will introduce customers to the newest and most up-to-date goods;
- the repair and sometimes alterations of goods;
- the provision of credit to certain customers;
- the exchange of goods returned by a customer as unsuitable.

The main types of shops are as follows:

- small shops (unit shops)
- department stores
- multiple or chain stores
- co-operative society retail shops
- self-service shops
- supermarkets
- hypermarkets.

Note. Modern developments have made the classifications outlined in this chapter less clear cut. For example, department stores have some 'self-selection' and specialist chains diversify into all sorts of goods. Again, the hypermarket tries to cater for under-one-roof shopping as in department stores, but with self-service, low prices and fast-moving goods. Despite these developments, each type of shop retains distinctive characteristics.

2.2   Small Shops

Small shops which have no branches, or very few, face fierce competition from their bigger rivals. In spite of this, the small retail business has survived remarkably well. There are several reasons for the small shop's popularity with shoppers.

1 Many small shopowners live 'on the premises', and their customers are neighbours. The shop may have the atmosphere

of a local club where first names are used and personal affairs are discussed . Many people prefer this friendly relationship to the much more impersonal atmosphere of big shops.

2 Personal acquaintance with customers enables the shopkeeper to provide informal credit. Purchases made during the week may be booked down and paid for at the end of the week.

3 Many small shops are situated away from the main shopping centres. In other words they are within walking distance of homes, offices and factories. It is handy for a shopper to obtain something without having to make a journey into town.

4 The owner of a small shop enjoys greater freedom for opening times. Big shops (which employ large numbers of assistants) are restricted in this respect by trade union regulations and the requirements of the Shops Act. The small shopkeeper does not usually employ assistants and so is not subject to legal restrictions on hours of opening. The small shop owner is willing to work long hours and often keeps the shop open when big shops are closed. Those people who are at work during the day enjoy the convenience of a shop that stays open in the evening or at weekends.

5 Small grocers may try to match the 'cut price' offers of the bigger shops. They do so by joining associations started by wholesalers called *voluntary chains*. Examples of voluntary chains include Spar, VG and Mace. The shopowners agree to buy as much as possible from the wholesaler who, through buying for all the shops in the chain, can obtain discounts for bulk buying from suppliers. These savings are passed on to the retailers who can make price reductions to meet the competition from bigger shops.

6 The growth of cash-and-carry wholesale warehouses has helped the small retailer. Under this self-service system a retailer pays at the door and takes the goods away in a van. The wholesaler does not have to provide delivery lorries, drivers, sales representatives or dispatch checkers. These savings permit goods to be offered at reduced prices and the retailer, in turn, can afford to lower prices to the public.

7 Some people consider that *franchising* has helped the small retailer to survive. Franchise agreements tend to vary in detail but in the basic essentials they are usually the same. Thus a retailer rents the name, product and operating method of a large company. In return for exclusive rights in a particular locality, the retailer makes a lump sum down payment as well as agreeing to pay a continuing percentage of the profits. The franchisee also undertakes to buy the product from the

company granting the franchise. Franchise businesses include food, car rental, drain cleaning and laundrettes.

2.3 Department Stores

A department store is a collection of shops under one roof. The aim is to provide in one building everything a customer might require. William Whiteley, who built up a huge store in London, boasted that he could supply anything from a flea to an elephant. Department stores still seek to attract shoppers by providing opportunities for a many-sided shopping expedition. They sell anything from clothes and furniture to groceries and electrical goods.

In addition to convenience, a department store provides comfort and luxury. Gordon Selfridge's ambition was to make his shop in Oxford Street the biggest attraction in London after Buckingham Palace and the Tower. He provided a restaurant, roof gardens and rest rooms, in addition to numerous sales departments. Shoppers were invited to enjoy the splendid premises and Selfridge declared his store was a social centre rather than a shop.

Department stores seek to attract customers by the provision of thickly carpeted floors, expensive decorations and fittings. Within their walls are travel agencies, restaurants, hairdressing salons and other facilities which attract shoppers.

Advantages

- A delivery service may be provided to allow customers to send orders by post or telephone.
- Credit accounts may be opened to enable customers to buy without having to pay cash on the spot.
- Shoppers can wander round the store at leisure without being pressed to purchase by assistants.

From the owners' point of view this kind of shop provides opportunities for big sales and profits, economies from bulk-buying and the benefits of employing experts in buying and selling.

Disadvantages

- The cost of the luxury facilities provided may cause prices to be higher than in some shops.

- In order to be economical a store needs to attract customers in large numbers. Only large towns which serve as shopping centres for wide areas can support department stores. Consequently stores have to be positioned where rents are high. The stores also rely upon quick and cheap transport facilities to bring shoppers from a wide area to shop.
- Compared with the small shop the atmosphere in a department store is rather impersonal and formal. Some people may prefer not to shop there for this reason.
- A store with a large number of departments presents management difficulties. For example, a store may have over 200 departments. Non-selling activities tend to grow up rapidly in such stores and only a minority of employees may be actually engaged in selling.
- A large number of credit sales involves a great deal of book-keeping and this cost adds to the already high overhead expenses (light, rent, rates, etc.).

Organisation

A typical department store has two main types of department: merchandise departments and service departments.

The merchandise departments sell the vast range of goods available in the store and the person in charge of a department is called a buyer. The term is misleading because the buyer is responsible not only for the purchase of stock but also for the sales policy of the department. In other words, the buyer manages the department.

The service departments support and supplement the merchandise departments. Three examples of service departments are: Clerical and Accounting; Receiving, Warehousing and Transport; Maintenance.

These departments are organised in a similar way to the merchandise departments, but the person in charge is termed a manager.

2.4   Multiple Shops

A multiple is a shop that has been multiplied until there is a chain stretching throughout a large area of the country. The size of its trade gives the multiple shop strong advantages over smaller rivals.

There are two types of chain organisation: the variety chain store and the specialist chain store. The variety chain store is divided into departments and sells a wide variety of goods (e.g. Marks and Spencer, Woolworth). The specialist chainstore concentrates on the sale of a narrower range of goods such as food, men's and women's wear, chemists' items or shoes. Examples of specialist chain stores are Sainsbury's, Next, Boots and Dolcis.

Multiples are well known in High Streets throughout the country, unlike the small shop which is only known locally.

General organisation of chain stores

The branch manager of a chain store has much less responsibility than the buyer in a department store. Buying, accounting, and selling prices are determined by the head office of the chain. Every month a return of sales made at each branch is sent to the head office, whilst cash from sales is paid into a local bank daily and sent to the head office's bank. The manager of the branch is concerned only with the day-to-day selling of goods. This policy of concentrating control of the chain in the head office is called *centralisation*. The advantages of this system are:

- purchases for the whole chain are so large that big discounts can be obtained from suppliers;
- specialists can be afforded for each job; buyers, accountants, window dressers and many other experts can be employed for their special skills.

Shoppers can see centralisation in the chain at work, because the shops are uniform in appearance and similar inside. Every detail, right down to the window displays in many cases, is planned by head office.

Advantages

- Bulk buying means buying more cheaply, so lower prices can be charged to customers. A chain which orders 100 000 cases of goods pays less per case than a shop ordering only 25. Consequently prices to customers can be lowered. Some firms such as Boots actually manufacture many of their own goods for sale. In this way the chain earns the maker's and wholesaler's profits in addition to the retailer's margin. Usually a chain's own brand of goods is offered in its shops at a lower price than an independent manufacturer's product.

- Nationwide branches of the same organisation mean that (*a*) stocks which are not selling well in one area may be transferred to another where demand is still high, and (*b*) all branches in the chain are not likely to suffer at the same time from a period of bad trade. For example, heavy unemployment in one part of the country may well reduce retail sales in the area, but branches in other regions can still be trading normally. Thus losses at a few branches can be carried while the chain as a whole is profitable. The multiple chain is in a very strong competitive position, therefore, compared with the small shopowner who would be forced out of business if trading losses occurred.

Disadvantages

- The major problem is that of controlling the activities of a large number of branches. The branch manager may be strictly controlled by head office and denied the freedom of action enjoyed by an independent retailer.
- Usually no credit is given, so that complicated bookkeeping can be avoided. Customers who cannot always pay cash may, therefore, be lost.
- The atmosphere of these shops is more impersonal than that of the small 'shop around the corner'. Consequently, some customers may prefer to shop locally rather than at the chain store in the High Street.

Variety chain stores

These stores are like other big shops in that they are found in all main shopping centres. Their organisation is similar to that of specialist chain stores but they differ in that they sell a very wide variety of goods. These include records, paint, make-up, food, toys, clothes, gardening tools and a host of other things. Some characteristics of variety chain stores are given below.

Open display

Variety chain stores display their goods on tray-like counter tops. Customers are able to select the goods they wish to buy and then hand them to the counter assistant for purchase.

Cheap prices

Low prices are typical of these stores.

Creative merchandising

Some large shops do not wait for manufacturers to produce items
before buying what they think will sell well in their stores.
Instead they go to the makers and assist in choosing and
designing the materials and the styles. This teamwork with the
factory is called *creative merchandising* and the articles may be sold
under the retailer's brand name.

The maker can plan production in the knowledge of an
assured market for the product. Savings in costs are passed on to
the retailer and reflected in the prices shoppers have to pay.

There are three ways, therefore, in which big multiple shops can
secure reduced prices:

1 bulk buying from independent manufacturers;
2 setting up their own factories;
3 working with manufacturers to produce goods made to the
retailer's own specification, i.e. creative merchandising.

2.5   Co-operative Societies

The first successful co-operative society was founded in 1844 by
a small group of working people who became known as the
Rochdale Pioneers. Though wages were low and living conditions poor, these people put all their savings together and set
up shop for themselves. Each took a turn in serving and any
profit made was divided up among the group. A member's share
of profit was known as a *dividend*. The amount was determined by
the sum spent in the shop. The greater the amount spent, the
larger the dividend received. In this way they provided the basic
necessities of life at prices below those asked in other shops. The
venture was successful and other societies grew up on the same
lines. Today there are co-operative retail societies throughout
the country. They vary in size from those in cities with membership around the million mark to those in villages with only a small
membership.

Organisation of the co-operative movement

The co-operative movement has a three-tiered structure.

1 The *Local Retail Societies*. Many have branches throughout
their area selling groceries and meat. The central premises in

the High Street may be in the form of a department store selling a wide range of articles. There may be supermarkets and self-service shops. Milk, bread and coal may be delivered to customers' homes.

2 The *Co-operative Wholesale Society (CWS)*. The Society makes bulk purchases from growers and manufacturers, and stocks and distributes goods for the retail societies. The latter buy from the CWS in the same way as a shopper buys from the local retail society. Dividends are paid to the retail societies on the basis of their purchases.

3 The *Co-operative Production Societies*. These are owned by the CWS and include tea plantations, dairies and a large number of factories making a wide range of consumer goods. The majority of goods sold by the retail societies are produced by the production societies.

Organisation of a retail society

Each society is in business on its own and the success or failure of one society does not concern the others.

In order to join a retail society a person must subscribe *share capital*. Shares earn a fixed rate of interest. Each member is then entitled to vote on decisions affecting the running of the society.

A *committee* is elected by the members to manage the society and appoint the management and staff. Meetings of members are held several times a year and each member has one vote.

The old dividend system has been replaced by *dividend stamps* which can be either changed for cash or goods *or* deposited in a share capital account. Some societies prefer to distribute profits by lowering prices.

Advantages

- A co-operative society has a private market consisting of its own members.
- The societies provide educational, social and welfare facilities for members and their families. Choirs, youth clubs, drama societies and similar activities are organised. The movement has its own political party, the Co-operative Party, which works closely with the Labour Party. These activities provide societies with a solid body of support in their trading.

In spite of the favourable factors mentioned above, and the attraction to customers of earning a dividend on purchases, the co-operative movement has tended to lose trade to other big shops. Why is this so?

Difficulties of the co-operative movement

- Some societies are too small to permit bulk buying. They cannot, therefore, obtain the advantage of large-scale operation which is enjoyed by their competitors, the multiples and supermarkets. (In order to improve their position, many societies have merged in recent years.)
- A proportion of the goods sold is from non-co-operative sources. The societies are, therefore, acting as distributing agents for their competitors.
- Most members do not exercise their right to attend meetings and vote. Consequently a society may be controlled, in effect, by a small number of members. The management committee may consist of people elected because of their loyalty to the ideals of the co-operative movement, rather than for their business abilities. Inefficiency in the society's business may continue unrecognised and the business experience necessary to compete successfully with other forms of retailing may be lacking.
- The bulk of the movement's share capital is supplied by the members who are free to withdraw their funds on demand. Large-scale withdrawals of shares may create capital problems, hence there is a basic potential weakness in the financial structure.

2.6   Self-Service

Self-service could reasonably be called do-it-yourself shopping. Traditionally the shop assistant finds the article asked for by the customer, wraps it, takes payment and returns any change. Self-service is quite different. Customers select what they need from all parts of the shop and make one payment to a cashier to cover the cost of all their purchases.

Advantages to the retailer

- The full range of goods is on show and their attractive display encourages 'impulse' buying (buying on the spur of the moment). Sales go up.

- The cost of assistants' wages can be reduced. Assistants are needed only to act as cashiers, to pre-pack and price goods, and to restock the shelves. Lower costs mean that prices can be cut in order to attract more customers.

Advantages to the customer

- People who go out to work have a very limited shopping time and waiting in a queue at a counter to be served can be exasperating. Self-service is much quicker and is a boon to people in a hurry.
- All goods are plainly on view and prices are clearly marked.
- Prices may be reduced.

Disadvantages to the retailer

- Losses through pilfering from the open shelves.
- The capital cost of changing over to self-service selling may be considerable.

Disadvantages to the customer

Self-service is not liked by all shoppers. Its main drawbacks are:
- the personal touch between assistant and customer is lost;
- no credit is given and there may be no delivery to customers' homes.

2.7   Supermarkets and Hypermarkets

Large self-service shops are known as supermarkets.

In the early days of self-service shopping, only groceries were sold in this way. They could be readily pre-packed, weighed, labelled and priced. However, the success of self-service selling, plus the discovery that a customer who was attracted by a particular article also bought others because they were on display, led to a broadening of the range. This trend was helped by an expansion in the production of packaged goods, for commodities that have to be weighed out are unsuitable for self-service trading. As a result, the supermarket appeared. These shops sell the full range of foods and household articles.

They step right across the traditional dividing lines between the grocery and other trades. The trades of the greengrocer, the butcher, the baker, the grocer and others have been merged by the supermarket.

The sales area is large, (a supermarket has a minimum selling area of 2000 sq ft (184 sq m) with three or more check-outs), and the largest supermarkets provide snack bars or coffee lounges where customers may enjoy a break from their shopping.

Supermarkets are popular with shoppers because:
- a high volume of sales and bulk-buying means prices are lower than in smaller shops;
- shoppers can buy a large number of their requirements in one shop (rather like the department store);
- customers are not hustled into buying by sales-conscious assistants.

Hypermarkets

The hypermarket is in many respects only a larger form of the supermarket. It, too, is based on self-service. There are, however, a number of important differences.

1 *Size* The hypermarket's total floor area is upwards of 50 000 sq ft (4645 sq m) and the variety of goods tends to be wider than in a supermarket. Besides foods, hypermarkets stock a huge range of items including clothes, electrical goods, bedding, car accessories, painting and decorating materials and toys.

2 *Position* A hypermarket is usually located on the edge of, or just outside, a town. Such sites are cheaper to buy or rent than town centre sites. The aim is to cater for the car-borne shopper and extensive car-parking facilities are provided. Unlike most supermarkets, a hypermarket offers shoppers the ease and comfort of shopping away from the crowded town centres.

3 *Price* Bulk purchases enable hypermarkets to set prices for many lines of goods below those of supermarkets and other shops. However, not everyone can benefit from the hyper-market's facilities. For example, elderly people may not wish to make the journey out of town to do their shopping, and people without a car may not find it easy to visit a hypermarket and take away their weekly shopping.

In France, Germany and America, the hypermarket has become a leading form of retail centre. It is, however, a relatively new development in Britain, because of considerable opposition based on two main points, namely the large amount of land required and the effect upon existing shopping centres.

The requirement for a large area of land on the edge of a town brings the hypermarket into conflict with the government's controls over building in green-belt areas. Also, a hypermarket could entail the development of an improved road system in the locality, again using up land. Opposition also arises from the fear that local authorities' income from rates could be affected if a hypermarket caused a decline in the number of shops in town centres.

2.8   Developments in Retailing

Technology

Scanning   Laser-scanning checkouts are appearing in large shops such as hypermarkets and supermarkets. The cashier uses a scanner to read the bar code on a customer's purchase. A computer instantly relays a description and price to the checkout where they are displayed on a screen and printed on the customer's receipt. The benefits to customers include itemised receipts and a speedier checkout operation (hitherto the cashier looked at each price label before ringing up each one on the till).

EFTPOS (Electronic Funds Transfer at Point of Sale)   This means using computer terminals in retail outlets to debit a customer's bank account using a plastic card, instead of money, cheques or credit card vouchers. At the same time, the retailer's account is credited. The adoption of EFTPOS should result in a speedier checkout process.

Home shopping

Experiments are under way in home shopping via viewdata systems (see page 191) or home computers.

Edge-of-town shopping centres

The number of large centres, such as the Metro-Centre in Gateshead, is growing. Inadequate car parking in many town centres has encouraged consumers to shop at these large sites, where cars can be parked and shopping needs can be met.

2.9 Some Retailing Terms

1 A *shopping precinct* is a shopping area closed off from traffic and with car parking facilities available.
2 Some shops sell certain goods at much below the market price. These special offers are called *loss leaders*. The retailer tries to attract customers by this means in the hope that once inside the shop, they will make further purchases. An example of a loss leader in a supermarket might be the offer of coffee at a very low price.
3 *Discount retailing* is widespread. Some discount shops are in shopping centres, but generally they are away from a town centre but near a main road. They sell cheaply because they buy in bulk and have low overhead expenses. Goods sold include food, drink, decorating and plumbing supplies, furniture and electrical goods.

Test Yourself

1 What are the functions of the retailer?
2 List the services provided by retailers for their customers.
3 How does the small shopkeeper survive in the face of competition from bigger shops?
4 Why do people enjoy shopping in department stores?
5 Briefly contrast the department store with the chain store.
6 What are the advantages and disadvantages of centralisation in the organisation of multiple stores?
7 Why is a chain of shops in a better competitive position than the small shopkeeper?
8 Name three distinctive features of variety chain stores.
9 Write down three ways in which big shops can secure reduced prices.
10 What is 'creative merchandising'?
11 Briefly outline the structure of a co-operative retail society.
12 Write down as many examples as possible of how a co-operative retail society differs from other forms of retailing.
13 Name the two sources of income enjoyed by the members of a co-operative retail society.

14 What criticisms are sometimes made of the co-operative movement?
15 Describe how a self-service shop differs from the traditional forms of retailing.
16 What are the advantages and disadvantages of self-service to the customer?
17 What are the advantages and disadvantages of self-service to the retailer?
18 Briefly outline the development of supermarkets.
19 Why are supermarkets popular with shoppers?
20 In what ways does a hypermarket differ from a supermarket?

Chapter 3

Retailing Without Shops

Retail trading can be carried on without shops. Selling which bypasses shops can take a number of forms. The main methods are:

- local retail markets;
- doorstep selling;
- mail order;
- automatic vending.

3.1 Markets

Most small country towns have market days when stalls are erected in the market-place and business is transacted in the open air. In some of the larger towns there are permanent covered retail markets, and there are many wholesale markets of this type too. The design of these covered markets is very varied and may be anything from a medieval stone building to the modern markets in many reconstructed city centres.

In the Middle Ages the right to hold a market or a fair was regarded as one of the most prized privileges that a lord or the king could grant a town. It meant that on certain fixed days, instead of peddling their wares from village to village, traders could invite their customers to visit them in the town. In time almost every important town acquired the right to hold a market.

While the right to hold markets was at first granted to Lords of the Manors, to monasteries, or to boroughs themselves by royal charter, since the middle of the 19th century a number of Acts of Parliament have been passed giving local authorities power to establish markets.

Retailers who sell at markets can hire stalls, and since it is usual for neighbouring market towns to have different market days, it is possible for a retailer to attend a number of markets each week.

Stall-owners do not have the same expenses as shop-keepers (for example, the latter pay heavy heating and lighting bills) and because their other overhead expenses are low, stall-owners can attract a wide custom by offering bargains.

Instead of selling in an established street market, some street traders set up their stalls or barrows along street kerbs, in car parks, or on pieces of waste land. Fruit and vegetables form a major proportion of sales. Newspapers, flowers, ice-cream, jewellery and food snacks are also sold in this way.

Fairs

Markets are usually held at least once a week, whereas fairs took place at longer intervals, perhaps only once a year, and in a more limited number of towns. In the Middle Ages fairs often had a religious association, being held annually on Saints' days. They were a means of developing trade and some fairs, such as the Nottingham Goose Fair, specialised in particular commodities.

Fairs survive today mainly in the form of the travelling amusement concerns, with roundabouts and side-shows, which in the past were attached to trade fairs. Nowadays the term 'fair' is sometimes applied to trade shows or exhibitions. Buyers and sellers attend from different countries and firms exhibit their goods. In Britain, fairs such as the Motor Show and the Boat Show attract many buyers from overseas.

3.2 Doorstep Selling

Some producers prefer to sell direct to consumers in their homes rather than through shops. Many types of product are sold direct, including plastic household containers, cleaning products and appliances, cosmetics and skin-care preparations, and lingerie.

A direct sales firm operates through a part-time sales force who sell either on a door-to-door basis or through selling 'parties' (coffee parties held in private houses to which friends and neighbours are invited).

The advantages to the producer of these forms of personal selling are:

- it enables the firm's representative to concentrate exclusively on the firm's products (in a shop, the assistant offers customers a variety of brands from which to choose);

- selling takes place in the familiar domestic setting of a private home or during a 'party' where the relaxed atmosphere encourages sales;
- goods can be made available for sale when shops are closed (as, for example, in the evening or at weekends).

Buyers also enjoy certain advantages. They include:

- the service of product demonstration at home;
- the facility of choosing products at their leisure without being rushed by sales-conscious shop assistants;
- guidance as to the suitability and quality of the merchandise.

On the other hand, at a party among neighbours and friends, consumers may find difficulty in refusing to buy. They may end up, therefore, with unwanted purchases.

Mobile Shops

Bakers, milkvendors, greengrocers and other tradespeople have called upon customers at their homes for many years. This old-established form of doorstep selling has been augmented by growing numbers of motor vehicles designed as shops and operating in many country districts and on new, isolated housing estates.

The great advantage to a householder is that the mobile shop stops outside the front door, so there is a saving in the time and effort of going out shopping and carrying goods home. Further, as long as a shop is on wheels, it is not classed as a place of business and so the mobile trader is not subject to the rules regarding closing hours – which benefits people who are out at work all day.

Choice, inevitably, is narrow because of the need to carry only popular, fast-selling lines of merchandise in order to make the most of the restricted space.

3.3   Mail Order

Many manufacturers and wholesalers have appreciated that the public find mail-order trading a convenient and trouble-free way to shop. Consequently they market their goods through this form of trading, while department stores and other retail shops adopt it in addition to their normal method of trading. Selling is organised on a direct-to-customer basis, usually by press advertisements.

In addition, there are the general mail-order firms which operate through part-time agents. The latter are employed to obtain orders and to collect payments from customers. Commission is received by agents on all orders.

In the mail-order business there is no personal contact between the seller and the buyer. The customer orders either from an advertisement in the daily press or from a catalogue. The latter is a large volume, often containing over 1000 pages and covering anything up to 20 000 items.

Very often the customer is given the opportunity of returning the goods if they are not satisfactory. Goods ordered in this way are said to be 'on approval'. If satisfied after inspecting the goods, the customer makes payment. Two other methods of purchase are:

1 *Cash with order*. If goods are returned by a customer, the mail-order firm will refund the purchase price. This guarantee is often expressed as 'satisfaction or money back'
2 *Cash on delivery*. Payment is made to the delivery-man/woman.

Advantages to customers

- It provides a supply of goods to people living in remote areas where there are very few shops. In a large country like the United States or Australia where long distances prevent many people from visiting shops, this type of trading is especially advantageous.
- When customers are sent a catalogue, they may be given the chance of becoming an agent, in which case they receive a commission on any goods sold.
- It offers products not normally stocked by the average retailer (for example, garages, sheds, and fencing are sold by this method).
- Customers are able to select their purchases from illustrated catalogues at leisure and in the privacy of their own homes. People who go out to work find it convenient to be able to sit down at home and do the shopping. In addition, traffic congestion, parking problems, and transport fares are all avoided.
- It provides easy and informal credit to attract those who cannot afford the full price at once.

- Merchandise can be viewed and handled before purchase. The system of sending goods on approval means that clothes can be tried on in the privacy of the home, and household furnishings and other equipment seen against the background in which they will be used.

Disadvantages to customers

- There is no personal contact between the seller and the customer.
- The expense of advertising tends to keep prices charged by mail-order firms rather higher than those charged in some shops.
- Customers may find difficulty in obtaining a clear idea of the quality or characteristics of goods from mail-order advertising.

Advantages to sellers

- Expensive shop sites are not required and business can be carried on from areas where rents are low.
- The newspaper-reading public provides a very wide market for mail-order business.
- Bulk orders with manufacturers mean that discounts can be obtained.
- The Post Office provides a parcels delivery service and facilities for payment by customers via (*a*) postal orders, (*b*) cash on delivery service (COD) and (*c*) Girobank payment. Parcel services are also provided by British Rail and other transport organisations.

Disadvantages to sellers

Against these advantages must be set the following drawbacks.

- Distribution costs are relatively high. Besides the cost of producing catalogues, advertising in newspapers, and the provision of credit, there is the payment of commission to agents. In addition the cost of 'bad debts' from people who do not pay up has to be met. Postage and packaging are further major expenses of mail-order firms.
- Large stocks incur the risk of heavy financial loss if goods go out of fashion or prices fall.

• If groups of workers like printers, postal or transport workers come out on strike, then the mail-order trade could be seriously affected.

3.4 Vending Machines

Automatic vending is the sale of goods by slot machines. Traditionally, the machines dispensed chocolate and cigarettes on sites at railway stations, airports and bus terminals. Today slot machines are found in many other places and the range of products sold by them has been extended. For instance, the range of goods sold by machines includes milk, hot and cold drinks, confectionery, and paperback books.

Retailers find that machines provide a useful addition to sales outside normal shopping hours. Another development has been the growth of machines installed in offices and factories. In some firms the canteen is organised on the automatic vending principle. Employees obtain change from the first machine to use in operating the machines selling food. Hot meals and salads, sandwiches and drinks can be bought.

Although automatic vending offers the buyer the advantage of convenience of buying for 24 hours each day, seven days a week, prices may be high. For instance, milk bought in this way costs more than having it delivered to the door. Usually the heavy capital cost of the machine causes this additional expense.

Slot machine selling offers one important advantage to the seller, especially in times of price cutting in the retail trade. The machine sells only at a given price, ensuring a constant profit margin on the goods sold.

Some people believe that eventually automatic vending will seriously challenge the retailer who provides personal service. Certainly, the growth of impersonal self-service and supermarket shopping suggests that this viewpoint has a sound basis.

Test Yourself

1 List four methods of shopping without shops.
2 Why are the prices of goods sold in local retail markets likely to be lower than ordinary shop prices?
3 List the main types of product sold by street traders.
4 What are the main differences between markets and fairs?
5 What is 'party selling'?

6 What are the advantages to consumers of 'party selling'?
7 Are there any disadvantages to consumers of this form of selling?
8 Write down the advantages and disadvantages of mobile shops to the customer.
9 What are the reasons for the increasing popularity of shopping by post?
10 Describe how the Post Office provides mail-order firms with facilities for (a) delivery (b) payment.
11 Write down the disadvantages incurred by a mail-order firm.
12 What incentives are there for a retailer to install an automatic vending machine?
13 List:
   (a) the places other than outside shops where vending machines are found
   (b) the range of products sold by vending machines.
14 Do you think automatic vending will ever replace the shopkeeper? Give reasons for your answer.

Chapter 4

Retailers and Suppliers

The retailer can purchase stock from either a *wholesaler* or a *manufacturer*. It is cheaper to buy direct from the manufacturer but usually impracticable. Manufacturers prefer to sell in bulk because of the high cost of packing, transporting and invoicing large numbers of small orders; many manufacturers fix a minimum quantity below which orders cannot be met. In addition, manufacturers give only short periods of credit, because cash is required as quickly as possible to finance further manufacture; most retailers lack sufficient capital to pay for large amounts of stock quickly. Consequently it is only the large-scale retailer with adequate storage space and capital who buys direct from manufacturers. Other retailers buy stock from a wholesaler. By so doing they can buy in relatively small quantities and also obtain the variety of stock which is essential for providing customers with a choice.

4.1 Documents Used

When a retailer purchases goods from a wholesaler, the transaction is recorded by a series of documents.

In practice these documents vary in style and layout, but the general principles involved in their use are the same. The illustrations in this chapter show the basic information provided by all commercial documents although the details on documents used by individual firms will vary. Whatever the form these documents take, they serve as written records of business transactions.

Letter of enquiry

A retailer who wishes to buy goods may write letters of enquiry to several wholesalers, asking for prices and terms of payment.

Catalogues and price lists

The wholesaler's catalogue will give details and illustrations of the goods sold by the wholesaler. The prices of the goods may be shown or they may be included in a separate *price list*. The use of separate price lists saves the expense of reprinting the catalogue whenever a price alters. Sometimes a *prices current* is issued which gives prices ruling at a certain date. The prices of some goods are subject to frequent changes so that it is impossible to issue a price list applicable for a period of time. A prices current gives the retailer an approximate idea of the ruling price and the actual price will be quoted when the order is placed.

Quotation

A reply from the wholesaler stating the price at which articles can be supplied is known as a quotation. It provides all the information required by the retailer, including price, terms of payment, the period of delivery and the terms of delivery.

The terms of payment may include trade and cash discounts.

Trade discount
This is a deduction made by the wholesaler from catalogue prices. The trade discount represents the retailer's *gross profit margin*. For example, a retailer may buy goods quoted by the wholesaler at £10 each, subject to a trade discount of 20%. Thus the retailer buys them for £8 each and sells them at £10, making a gross profit on each article of £2.

The wholesaler may vary the amount of trade discount to allow for changes in prices, and so avoid the expense of reprinting catalogues. For example, if trade discount is at present 20%, prices can be increased by reducing it to 15%. Similarly, catalogue prices can be lowered by increasing the trade discount from 20% to 25%.

Cash discount
This is a reduction in the *net price* of the goods (that is the catalogue price less trade discount) offered by wholesalers to encourage prompt payment.

The prompt settlement of bills enables suppliers to pay their own creditors, purchase more stock, or earn interest by investing the money. Another reason for giving cash discount is that prompt settlement saves the supplier some clerical work. When payment is made in small amounts over a period of some months, the supplier has to keep written records of these payments. In addition, a supplier may have to correspond with debtors to request settlement of the amounts owing. This extra work is an additional cost whereas quick payment avoids the expense.

Cash discounts also offer certain advantages to retailers. By paying promptly, substantial savings may be made on the cost of large orders. In addition, prompt settlement earns a customer the reputation of being a 'good payer'. If goods became scarce for any reason, it is likely that suppliers would give preference to customers who have proved themselves to be good payers.

Cash discount will vary with the *period of credit* allowed by the wholesaler. For example, if payment is made within seven days, a cash discount of 5% may be offered, but only 2.5% after that up to a maximum of 28 days. The terms of payment do not always provide for cash discount, in which case the terms are *net*.

The period of delivery
This may be quoted in the following terms:

- *ready delivery* i.e. the wholesaler has the goods in stock and they will be sent when an order is received;
- *prompt delivery* i.e. delivery can be made within a few days of the order being received;
- *forward delivery* i.e. goods are not in stock and the wholesaler cannot give an actual delivery date at present. When a date can be quoted, the retailer will be informed.

Terms of delivery
These are used in the quotation to indicate whether the retailer or wholesaler is to pay for the cost of packing and delivery of the goods. They include the following:

- *carriage paid* i.e. the wholesaler pays for packing and delivery charges (carriage paid is often quoted on orders above specified amount as an incentive to the retailer to place large orders).
- *carriage forward* i.e. the retailer pays for packing and delivery charges (carriage forward is usually quoted for small orders);
- *for (free on rail)* i.e. the wholesaler pays the cost of transporting the order from a warehouse to the nearest railway station. All other costs are payable by the retailer.
- *ex-warehouse* i.e. all costs after goods leave the warehouse must be paid by the retailer. The is another method of indicating that the buyer has to pay carriage.

After comparing the quotations received from wholesalers, the retailer decides which is the most acceptable and then sends an order.

The order

The purpose of an order is to provide a clear statement of the quantity and type of goods required. The use of *reference numbers* in a catalogue makes the identification of the goods more certain.

Fig. 4.1   *An order*

QUANTITY	GOODS	COST

A. RETAILER LTD.
The High Street, Solihull SO1 9UL

A.S. Wholesale Ltd
70 Warehouse Road
Birmingham B13 4AM

ORDER NO
A/ 88201

Please supply   Date   2 September 19—

QUANTITY	GOODS	COST
100 Boxes	Ready salted crisps (List No. 91)	£2.00 per box.
100 Boxes	Oxo flavoured crisps (List No. 93)	£2.00 per box.
200 Boxes	Chicken flavoured crisps (List No. 94)	£2.00 per box.
	Delivery Instructions: Prompt delivery carriage paid	SIGNED......................

If the order is the first received by the wholesaler from a particular retailer, enquiries will be made about the retailer's *credit-worthiness* before the goods are sent on credit terms. A retailer may be asked, therefore, for the names of *referees*: that is, persons to whom reference may be made regarding the retailer's integrity in business. The retailer may provide two kinds of reference: a bank reference or a trade reference.

Bank reference
The retailer gives the name of a bank. Bankers know something about the financial integrity of their customers but a bank will

supply information only to another banker. It will be necessary, therefore, for the wholesaler to ask a bank manager to obtain a reference from the retailer's bank.

Trade reference
The retailer may give as reference the name of another wholesale firm with which trading has taken place.

If neither of these methods provides the wholesaler with the information required, a *status enquiry agency* (also known as a *credit reference agency*) can be approached. In return for a fee, particulars of the firm concerned will be supplied.

If, as a result of these enquiries, the wholesaler decides that credit cannot be offered, the retailer will be asked for payment before the order is dispatched. This is done by sending a *pro forma invoice* which serves as a request for payment before goods are sent (see page 39).

Dispatch documents

Assuming that the wholesaler is satisfied with the replies from inquiries made, the order can be packed and dispatched.

There are three documents concerned with the dispatch of an order: the *advice note*, the *delivery note* and the *consignment note*. It is unlikely that all three documents will be used in a particular transaction. Very often the advice note is not necessary because the invoice can be sent as soon as the goods are dispatched. In this case the invoice gives notification to the retailer of the dispatch of the goods, as well as serving its purpose as the bill.

Advice note
This document is sent at the time that the goods are dispatched .
Its purpose is to notify the retailer that the goods are on the way.
It lists details of the goods (except for the price), the date of dispatch, the method of dispatch and the terms of dispatch.

Delivery note
This document, which also gives a list of the goods without showing their prices, may be sent with the parcel of goods. Its purpose is to assist the retailer to check the goods on arrival. Where a business has its own delivery van, a duplicate copy will be given to the driver and is signed by the recipient as proof of delivery.

Prices are omitted from advice notes and delivery notes so that the retailer's assistants can check goods without learning their cost price. This information is the concern of the owner of the business and no-one else.

Consignment note
This document is supplied by the transport undertaking. The wholesaler enters details of the goods to be dispatched and the name and address of the retailer to whom the goods are being sent. The consignment note accompanies the goods during the journey and the retailer will sign it as a record of delivery.

The invoice

The invoice or bill sent by the wholesaler states:

- quantity of goods
- description of goods
- prices
- method of delivery
- terms of delivery
- amount of trade discount
- terms of payment
- VAT information.

The invoice provides a summary of a transaction between the wholesaler and the retailer, and the purpose of the document is to notify the retailer of the amount due.

An invoice often has the abbreviation *E and OE* (*errors and omissions excepted*) printed on it. The purpose is to safeguard the supplier against loss from any mistake. For example, if a mistake has been made in calculating the amount owing on the invoice, the supplier reserves the right to correct the mistake.

Value added tax (*VAT*) is a tax payable on any goods and services which fall within its scope. It is assessed on the value which a trader adds to goods and services during a particular stage of the production process. Certain goods and services are *exempt* from VAT and so the seller does not charge the tax on sales. Some other classes of goods and services are *zero-rated*, which means they are technically taxable but at a nil rate. Thus no VAT is charged on their sale.

Fig. 4.2 *An invoice*

QUANTITY	GOODS	PRICE			

A.S. WHOLESALE LTD.
70 Warehouse Road, Birmingham B13 4AM

To: A. Retailer Ltd
  The High Street
  Solihull SO1 9UL
  Order No. A/88201

INVOICE NO
Z 291

Date 5 September 19—

QUANTITY	GOODS	PRICE			
100 Boxes	Ready salted crisps (List No. 91)	£2	00	200	00
100 Boxes	Oxo flavoured crisps (List No. 93)	£2	00	200	00
200 Boxes	Chicken flavoured crisps (List No. 94)	£2	00	400	00
				800	00
	Less trade discount 25%			200	00
				600	00
	Terms Net Plus VAT: 15%			90	00
E & O E	Delivery carriage paid.			690	00

Note. Traders registered with HM Customs and Excise for VAT purposes are obliged to provide information on invoices showing VAT rates, amounts and registration numbers. A VAT registration number is supplied by HM Customs and Excise who collect VAT and to whom at regular intervals the trader makes a tax return.

The pro forma invoice
This is exactly the same as an ordinary invoice except the words *pro-forma* (which mean *as a matter of form*) are stamped on it.
    A pro forma invoice may be used in the following circumstances:

- as a request for payment before goods are dispatched, e.g. when the wholesaler has received an order from a retailer to whom credit cannot be offered;
- as a reply to the retailer asking for a quotation from a wholesaler. The document indicates what the actual invoice would be like if an order is placed.

The credit note

A credit note is sent by the wholesaler to the retailer if it is necessary to reduce the amount charged on the invoice. This can happen in the following circumstances:

- when the retailer has been overcharged;
- when the retailer returns damaged goods or goods sent by the wholesaler in error;
- when packing-cases, which have been charged to the retailer on the invoice, are returned.

Credit notes are usually printed in red in order to distinguish them from other documents.

Fig. 4.3 *A credit note*

	A.S. WHOLESALE LTD.	
	70 Warehouse Road, Birmingham B13 4AM	
To: A. Retailer Ltd		**CREDIT NOTE NO**
The High Street		C 92
Solihull SO1 9UL		
		Date 10 September 19—

QUANTITY	GOODS	NET PRICE
4 Boxes	Ready salted crisps (List No. 91)	
	returned damaged 7 September 19—.	
	Invoice No. Z 291	£8.00
	Less trade discount of 25%	£2.00
		£6.00
	Plus VAT: 15%	£0.90
		£6.90

The debit note

A debit note is sent by the wholesaler to the retailer if it is necessary to increase the sum charged on the invoice. This may be necessary if the retailer has been undercharged.

Some firms prefer to deal with an undercharge or overcharge to a customer by sending a *corrected invoice*.

The statement

At the end of each month, the wholesaler sends to the retailer a *statement of account* showing the following items:

- any unpaid balance still owing to the wholesaler at the *beginning* of that month from earlier months;
- totals of invoices sent out during the month;
- credits for any allowances;
- debits for any undercharges;
- amounts of cash received;
- the unpaid balance.

The statement shows the terms of payment for the sum owing on the month's transactions. The purpose of this document is to request payment for the sum owing.

Fig. 4.4   *A statement*

DATE	DETAILS	DEBIT		CREDIT		BALANCE	
	A.S. WHOLESALE LTD. 70 Warehouse Road, Birmingham B13 4AM To: A. Retailer Ltd The High Street Solihull SO1 9UL **STATEMENT** 3 October 19—						
19—	A/c Rendered						
1 Sept.	To Balance owing					149	
4 Sept.	By Cheque			149			
5 Sept.	Invoice No Z 291	690				690	
10 Sept.	Credit Note No. C 92			6	90	683	10
12 Sept.	Invoice No. Z 403	75				758	10
19 Sept.	Invoice No. Z 614	98				856	10
26 Sept.	Invoice No. Z 906	104				960	10
	TERMS Net					THE LAST AMOUNT IN THIS COLUMN IS THE AMOUNT OWING	

The retailer will check the statement with the invoices, credit notes and debit notes received from the wholesaler. If all is in order, the retailer will send to the wholesaler a cheque in settlement of the account, after deducting the sum allowed for cash discount. If payment is delayed beyond the period for which cash discount is allowed the retailer will have to pay the amount owing in full.

The receipt

The wholesaler acknowledges payment of the account by issuing a receipt. The latter is dated and shows the sum paid, by whom, and who received it. It has become the practice for businesses receiving payment by cheque not to issue receipts unless requested to do so. The cheque itself constitutes a receipt when cleared by the paying banker.

4.2   Stock Control

In retailing (as in other kinds of trading) a systematic method of stock control is necessary to ensure that purchases can be planned and kept in line with sales. Buying and selling are so closely related that it is difficult to separate them as functions. On the skill of the one depends the success of the other.

There are two types of stock control. The first is through a *merchandise budget*. This is a planned scheme of spending by which sales, and the stock needed to make them, are estimated at least six months in advance. These calculations have to be adjusted as the year progresses in order to fit in with the results of actual trading.

The second system is called *unit stock control*. This is a daily check on stock lines to find out their rate of sale and the most popular colours, sizes, styles and so on. Thus re-ordering can be carefully planned to meet demand and goods should never be out of stock.

Slow-moving stocks

Generally, retailers prefer to concentrate on quick-selling lines. If the *rate of turnover* (that is, the number of times the average stock is sold during any given period) can be increased, then total sales over a period will also increase. An increase in sales often results in an increase in profit. Thus lines of stock which sell very slowly are probably not worth stocking. The main causes of slow-moving stocks are briefly discussed below.

Bad planning
Unless the retailer buys stock in exact proportion to consumers' demand, there will inevitably be some investment of capital in merchandise which either does not sell at all or at best sells very slowly.

Shop-soiled goods
Shop soilage is both the cause and the result of slow-moving stocks. There are a number of ways in which goods can become dirty or damaged. For example, a shortage of storage space may result in goods being crammed carelessly so that they soon lose their new appearance. Similarly, careless handling of goods by assistants or by customers causes shop soilage. Stock depreciation is caused in certain circumstances by the effects of light, heat and damp.

4.3 Sales Events

Many retailers who deal in seasonable goods, such as clothing, divide their year into two periods, namely the summer and winter seasons. Each period ends with a bargain sale in which old stock which has not sold well can be cleared before the new season's lines arrive.

Only a proportion of the merchandise in a sale is *marked down* from existing stock. (If there is a large amount of stock reduced in price to clear it suggests that there has been bad buying by the retailer, or poor stock-keeping.) Therefore in addition to reductions on, for example, small and large sizes of garments, or on goods at either end of a range, there may be bargains in the form of manufacturers' and wholesalers' end-of-season surplus stocks, and factory *imperfects* or *seconds*. These are bought in at sales times in order to attract customers seeking bargains.

As well as providing storage space and making capital available for new stock, a sale acts as an advertisement for the business and encourages shoppers to buy at a period of the year when trade is slack.

Test Yourself

1 What is the purpose of a letter of enquiry?
2 Write down ways in which a wholesaler may reply to a letter of enquiry.

3 Name two uses of trade discount.
4 What is the purpose of cash discount?
5 Write down the meaning of the following terms: ready delivery, prompt delivery, forward delivery.
6 What does 'ex-warehouse' mean?
7 Name two kinds of reference that a retailer may provide for a wholesaler.
8 How does an advice note differ from a delivery note?
9 Why are prices omitted from advice notes and delivery notes?
10 What is the purpose of an invoice?
11 Name the tax which may appear on an invoice.
12 Who collects this tax from traders?
13 Name two uses of a pro forma invoice.
14 Why does the wholesaler sometimes send credit notes to retailers?
15 What is the purpose of a debit note?
16 What is the purpose of a monthly statement?
17 Which document is used to acknowledge payment?
18 Name two types of stock control.
19 What are the main causes of slow-moving stocks?
20 How are 'Sales' and stock control related to each other?

Chapter 5

Wholesale Trade

The aim of *production* is to satisfy consumers' *wants*. The production process is incomplete, therefore, until goods actually reach persons who want them. The usual route by which goods reach the consumer from the producer is by way of the wholesaler and retailer. The function of the latter as the last link in the chain of distribution was considered in Chapters 2 and 3.

5.1 Services of Wholesalers

A wholesaler (known also as a *merchant, factor* or *distributor* in some trades) deals in *whole* or *bulk* units. The wholesale trade serves as a connecting link between:

(*a*) the producer of raw materials and the manufacturer;
(*b*) the manufacturer and the retailer.

Thus the wholesale trade provides services to the producer of raw materials, the manufacturer and the retailer.

Producers of raw materials

The majority of raw materials are imported and wholesalers purchase supplies as they arrive in the country. In addition, wholesalers deal with home-produced raw materials. Their aim is to find *markets* for both.

Commodity exchanges provide meeting places where importers sell raw materials to wholesalers. Examples are the Wool Exchange and the Baltic Exchange in the City of London. The Baltic Exchange is a leading European market for grain. Dealings in vegetable oil and seeds of all kinds also take place there.

45

Manufacturers

Wholesalers provide a wide range of services for manufacturers.

1 They provide supplies of raw material obtained from home and overseas.
2 They save manufacturers a great deal of time and work by making bulk purchases for them. If there were no wholesalers, the retailer would have to buy directly from the manufacturer. Thus every manufacturer would have to send a sales representative to visit every retailer to demonstrate products. Suppose, for example, that a retailer buys stock from 10 manufacturers who in turn deal with a total of 400 retailers. The paperwork involved in these transactions is as follows:

(*a*) orders from 400 retailers to 10 manufacturers = 4000
(*b*) invoices from 10 manufacturers
    to 400 retailers = 4000
(*c*) statements of account from 10 manufacturers
    to 400 retailers = 4000
(*d*) cheques from 400 retailers to 10 manufacturers = 4000
            Total number of documents = 16000

This volume of paperwork has to be financed by payments to clerical staff, suppliers of stationery etc. However, if one representative from a wholesaler visits each retailer in turn to collect orders, which are then combined in one large order from the wholesaler to the manufacturer, the paperwork is as follows:

(*a*) orders from 1 wholesaler to 10 manufacturers 10
(*b*) invoices from 10 manufacturers to 1 wholesaler 10
(*c*) statements of account from 10 manufacturers
    to 1 wholesaler 10
(*d*) cheques from 1 wholesaler to 10 manufacturers 10
            Total number of documents 40

(*a*) orders from 400 retailers to 1 wholesaler 400
(*b*) invoices from 1 wholesaler to 400 retailers 400
(*c*) statements of account from 1 wholesaler
    to 400 retailers 400
(*d*) cheques from 400 retailers to 1 wholesaler 400
            Total number of documents 1600

When the wholesaler is used there are 1640 items of paperwork involved compared with 16 000 items when manufacturers deal directly with retailers. By using the wholesaler, a manufacturer is saved a great amount of clerical work.

In addition, the manufacturer is saved the trouble and expense of dispatching a large number of very small parcels to retailers. The use of the wholesaler saves a manufacturer packing costs and transport charges.

3 Manufacturers prefer to dispose of their output as quickly as possible, since many do not possess storage facilities for large quantities of goods. The wholesaler relieves the manufacturer of storage difficulties by storing finished products in a warehouse until they are required.

4 Wholesalers collect orders from a large number of retailers and, in the course of their work, they gain a knowledge of the state of the market. Wholesalers are able, therefore, to inform manufacturers of any changes in the demand for their products.

5 Generally a manufacturer is not prepared to give credit to customers. Manufacturers require large sums of cash every week in order to pay employees' wages. Consequently they prefer to sell goods for cash. If goods were sold straight to retailers, a long period of credit would be necessary to allow some goods to be sold before payment is made. The wholesaler pays for goods as soon as they are received and saves the manufacturer from having capital 'tied up' in stock for long periods.

Retailers

1 The wholesaler makes bulk purchases from manufacturers and sells to retailers in smaller quantities. Retailers may, therefore, draw upon the wholesaler's stocks at convenient times and save the expense of maintaining large stocks and storage facilities at their premises. They can maintain a small stock of many individual items and so display an attractive range of goods.

2 The wholesaler stocks the products of a large number of manufacturers and retailers are provided with a wide range of choice. They are saved the time and expense of visiting or ordering from a large number of manufacturers.

3 Many retailers operate on only a small amount of capital and the wholesaler helps to finance a stock of goods by allowing a long period of credit. Thus a retailer can expect to sell goods

before paying for them. If stocks were purchased direct from manufacturers, larger orders would be necessary and a very short period of credit would be allowed by the manufacturer. Under such conditions a retailer would require a greater amount of capital.

4 As the connecting link between manufacturer and retailer, wholesalers are in a position to give valuable advice to the retailer. For instance they will provide, through their representatives, catalogues and price lists, details of new fashion trends, new products etc., They may also supply retailers with window display material.

5 At one time wholesalers used to weigh and re-pack such commodities as sugar for the convenience of retailers. Most goods are pre-packed by the manufacturer these days and small packets in larger packages are sent out to wholesalers. However, some wholesalers may undertake the preparation of the commodity for sale to retailers. Thus a wholesale tea merchant may purchase many kinds of tea, blend them, and pack the tea ready for sale. Some wholesale grocers perform a task in processing food by grinding coffee and smoking bacon.

5.2 Warehouses

Wholesale warehouses are needed to store commodities for several reasons.

1 Most goods are produced ahead of demand and warehouses are required for storage during the interim period. Warehousing enables manufacturers to concentrate on making goods and selling in bulk to wholesalers without having to cope with the problems of storage or retailing.

2 Many commodities are seasonal. Raw materials arrive at British ports only at certain times during the year. For example, cotton is imported during the summer months and warehoused until required by manufacturers throughout the year. In the case of agricultural products, harvests take place at different times in different parts of the world. Warehousing ensures that food supplies are available to consumers throughout the year.

3 Warehousing avoids large fluctuations in prices. The holding of stocks by wholesalers means that a sudden increase in demand by consumers can be met, by retailers quickly replenishing their stocks. Without large 'buffer' stocks in ware-

houses, a sudden increase in demand would lead to scarcity and a rapid rise in price. Similarly if demand falls, a policy of carefully limiting releases from warehouses can moderate the fall in price.

Location

A wholesale warehouse should be situated:

- where it is easily accessible to retailers from a wide area;
- where good transport facilities exist.

The wholesaler may operate a fleet of vans for the delivery of orders and the warehouse may be situated, therefore, on the outskirts of a town and away from time-wasting traffic congestion. On the other hand, advantage may be taken of rail and road facilities if these are available.

Usually the warehouse is not such an attractive establishment as the retailer's shop. The latter occupies a prominent position in a shopping centre and is decorated and equipped in order to attract custom. The wholesaler's warehouse can be in a back street so long as the location is satisfactory for serving the surrounding district. Most retailers rarely visit the warehouse and those who do are not interested in the appeal of the premises. Compared with a retailer the wholesaler invests less capital in premises and equipment. Instead much more is invested in stocks of goods.

Organisation

The organisation of a wholesale warehouse depends largely upon the nature of the business, but the main divisions are outlined below.

Commodity departments

When a wide variety of goods are handled, each commodity or group of commodities will form a separate department. For example, a drapery warehouse will have a large number of departments. On the other hand, a furniture warehouse may only have one selling department.

Each department is in the charge of a buyer who is responsible to the managing director for the success of the department. Under the control of the buyer are the sales staff who deal with orders from retailers making personal visits, or with orders received by post. Sales representatives visit retailers for the purpose of collecting orders.

Purchasing department
The work of this department is to deal with orders for stock from the commodity departments. Orders will be placed with manufacturers and importers.

Receiving department
When goods that have been ordered arrive, they will be checked in this department and then sent to the appropriate commodity department to be taken into stock. Details of goods received will be forwarded to the accounts department.

Accounts department
The work of this department is twofold. It deals, first, with prompt cash payments *to* manufacturers and secondly, it handles payments *from* retailers. Before an order from a retailer is packed and dispatched, the total value will be checked in this department to see that the amount does not exceed the credit allowed to the retailer.

Packing and dispatch department
When a retailer's order is received, copies are made and forwarded to the appropriate commodity departments. Each department sends goods to the packing and dispatch department where as they are parcelled up into one consignment, checked against a copy of the order and dispatched.

Publicity department
This department is responsible for seeing that the goods stocked are advertised to retailers in the appropriate trade journals. Price lists and catalogues are also circulated to retailers.

5.3   Voluntary Chains and Groups

The small retail business is faced with ever-increasing competition from multiple stores and supermarkets. These large retailers purchase in such large quantities that they can cut out the wholesaler and buy direct from manufacturers. Consequently wholesalers as well as small retail businesses have suffered from the growth of large shops. They have a mutual interest in helping one another, and many wholesalers have invited small shops to link together in voluntary chains and groups. Members of each organisation display a common advertising symbol.

A group consists of one wholesaler and a number of retailers, whereas a voluntary chain consists of several wholesalers and a much larger number of retailers. The names of voluntary chains include VG, Mace, and Spar. The organisation of a chain and a group is broadly similar. Retailers guarantee to make a large proportion of their purchases with a particular wholesaler who enjoys the certainty of a fixed quantity of business. The wholesaler saves the expense of sending out representatives to obtain orders and keep in touch with these retailers. In addition, delivery costs and clerical costs are reduced. In return the wholesaler offers retailers goods at reduced prices and provides other services such as group advertising on television and in national and local newspapers. Retailers in voluntary chains and groups enjoy the advantages of *bulk buying* which enables them to compete with large stores.

5.4 Cash-and-Carry Wholesaling

In the 1960s a few wholesalers began a cash-and-carry service for retailers and this form of wholesaling has grown rapidly.

The essence of cash-and-carry or *self-service wholesaling* is the elimination of credit, deliveries, loading expenses, sales representatives and invoicing. These savings in the wholesaler's costs permit a reduction in prices so that the small retailer can compete effectively with the supermarkets. The retailer may make as many visits a week to the cash-and-carry warehouse as necessary. Consequently the amount of capital invested in stock is reduced. Cash-and-carry has expanded from groceries into non-food lines such as textiles.

5.5 The Co-operative Wholesale Society

The co-operative movement has its own wholesale organisation which supplies the co-operative retail societies with the stocks they need. The retail societies receive a dividend on purchases from the CWS and the latter sells also to non-co-operative retailers.

The CWS operates a large number of factories making a range

of consumer goods which includes clothes, foodstuffs and furniture. In addition the CWS has extensive farming and meat-freezing interests. It also owns a bank, which has branches in many large towns and cities, and it operates travel and insurance services.

5.6 Intermediaries

Retailers and wholesalers are often described as intermediaries or *middlemen*. The term can be used to describe anyone who comes between the *producer* and the *consumer*. An intermediary may be known as an agent, factor, broker, dealer, merchant or speculator. Whatever the name given to these intermediaries, they share a common function in assisting the flow of goods from producer to consumer.

In the home trade the number of intermediaries engaged in the distribution of a product depends on the particular character of the trade concerned. In some trades a single wholesaler provides the link between producer and retailer; in others, there may be two or more. For example, in trades where there are large numbers of retailers with relatively small total sales (such as groceries and provisions, or tobacco and cigarettes) it may be impossible for large-scale wholesalers to meet their needs. Thus smaller wholesalers buy from regional wholesalers and supply retailers in their local areas.

In foreign trade, the number of intermediaries tends to be greater than in the home trade because there are more specialist functions to be performed. Many of these middlemen never own or handle the goods in which they deal. *Import merchants, export merchants* and *brokers* are examples of intermediaries engaged in foreign trade. Import merchants, for example, arrange ware-housing for consignments of goods from abroad and their subsequent sale on a commodity exchange. This work is carried out by brokers who act as agents for buyers and sellers. Buyers include manufacturers and wholesalers who wish to buy supplies of raw material, and the sellers are the producers or growers of the commodity.

Intermediaries are frequently blamed for the difference that may exist between the farm or factory price and the price paid by consumers. It is certainly true that each middleman who deals with the goods has to make a profit. Thus goods are sold at every stage at a price higher than that paid for them. However, the retailer is not compelled to buy stock from a wholesaler; neither is a manufacturer required to sell to the wholesaler rather than direct to retailers. Thus, the fact that many retailers and manufacturers deal voluntarily with wholesalers rather than direct with one another indicates that the wholesaler provides valuable services to both of them.

The greater the amount of *specialisation* that is introduced into distribution, the greater will be the number of intermediaries employed between producer and retailer. Greater division of labour in distribution should mean more efficient distribution, just as in industry greater division of labour achieves more efficient output. Consequently when middlemen are specialists performing a necessary service, their work reduces the cost of distribution rather than increasing it.

5.7 Direct Dealing

Although most manufactured products reach the retailer through a wholesaler, there are a number of examples where the manufacturer deals direct with the retailer or even with customers.

Direct dealing between manufacturer and retailer occurs in the instances outlined below.

Large-scale retailers

Multiple shops and department stores often deal direct with the manufacturers. Their sales are so big that their orders are as large as those of a wholesale firm.

Manufacturers of branded goods

Many makers of branded goods distribute their products direct to retailers in order to ensure that their products reach as many shops as possible. An independent wholesaler may not promote the sale of an article as strongly as the manufacturer would like. Hence manufacturers of branded goods prefer, where possible, to distribute direct to retailers.

Where technical knowledge is of importance

Manufacturers of office equipment, for instance, employ representatives with expert knowledge who deal directly with the consumer. The makers of equipment or machinery may undertake *after-sales-service*: that is, they may offer to service and repair their products.

In spite of some exceptions, wholesaling is an essential part of the work of production. When the wholesaler is cut out, someone else has to do the wholesaler's work. For example, large shops which deal direct with manufacturers have to provide warehouses for their large stocks of goods. Increasingly, this is provided by transport firms. 'Just-in-time' delivery permits retailers to make maximum effective use of space in stores. Similarly, a transport firm might handle storage and distribution for a manufacturer.

Test Yourself

1 Explain briefly how wholesaling forms part of the production process.
2 The wholesale trade links the producer of raw materials and the _____.
3 Write down five services performed by the wholesaler for the manufacturer.
4 Why are wholesale warehouses needed?
5 Give two factors to consider in the location of a warehouse.
6 (a) In a wholesale warehouse the goods are on display in _____ departments.
  (b) Cash payments to manufacturers and sums received from retailers are dealt with in the _____ department.
  (c) On arrival, goods from manufacturers are checked in the _____ department.
  (d) Advertising of the goods handled by the warehouse is the work of the _____ department.
7 What is the difference between a voluntary group and a voluntary chain?
8 Why were voluntary groups and chains formed?
9 Give three examples of voluntary chains.
10 How does the cash-and-carry system reduce a wholesaler's costs?
11 What major advantage is enjoyed by retail co-operative societies over independent retailers?
12 What is an intermediary or middleman?

13 Do middlemen cause prices to be higher than would otherwise be the case?
14 In direct dealing, the _____ is bypassed.
15 Give two examples of direct dealing.

Chapter 6

Markets

The process of distributing goods to consumers necessitates a number of *exchanges*. For example, the wholesaler buys from manufacturers and sells to retailers; the retailer purchases stock either from a wholesaler or direct from a manufacturer and sells to consumers. Whenever exchange takes place between buyers and sellers a *market* is in operation.

The word 'market' is often used to refer to a particular place where buyers and sellers meet regularly. For example, the weekly market held in country towns for the sale of local produce; the wholesale fruit, vegetable and flowers market at Nine Elms in London; the market for stocks and shares at a stock exchange, and so on. However, while markets are often found in particular places, the development and use of communications in modern times has made the gathering of buyers and sellers in one place less necessary. Worldwide markets exist in commodities such as oil and steel.

6.1 Types of Markets

Markets exist for all commodities and for all services. For example, there are financial markets, commodity markets and markets for consumer goods. *Financial markets* include the market in ownership of company shares (see page 92) and the market in foreign currencies (see page 146). *Commodity markets* are often held in a particular place or building. Many of the old-established commodity exchanges for raw materials and foodstuffs are found in London, but there are also important markets for cotton, fruit and corn in provincial centres such as Liverpool and Manchester. Commodity markets are conducted by *brokers* who act as agents for principals who are buyers and sellers. Buyers include manufacturers and wholesalers, while sellers are the producers or growers of the commodity.

Markets for *consumer goods* are formed by the wholesale and retail trades. In the *retail market* the finished product is made available to consumers. The simplest form of retail market is the street market which is held regularly in many towns and villages on certain days. The permanent retail market is formed by the various kinds of shops.

The *wholesale market* extends over a much wider area than the retail market. Orders received from retailers by the wholesaler are passed on to the manufacturer and communication may take place by telephone and letter. There may be no central meeting-place for buyers and sellers other than the showrooms maintained by wholesalers and manufacturers for those of their customers who are in the locality.

Consumers' and producers' goods

Goods can be classified as either consumers' or producers' goods. The latter are goods used to assist the production of other goods. For example, factory buildings, machinery, means of transport, and raw materials, are all *producers' goods*. Producers' goods have to be distributed from the producers to those manufacturers who require them.

Consumers' goods, on the other hand, are products in the form in which consumers wish to have them. They can be grouped in two ways, namely, foodstuffs and manufactured goods. Consumers' goods are made available to shoppers through the various kinds of retail establishments and so distribution among the various types of retailers is necessary.

Thus three different channels of distribution can be distinguished:

- manufactured goods
- agricultural commodities
- raw materials.

6.2 Manufactured Goods

The normal channel by which goods reach the consumer from the maker is through the *wholesaler* and the *retailer*.

Some manufacturers deal directly with the retailer, particularly those large-scale retailers whose orders may be as large as those of some wholesalers. As noted on page 53, *direct dealing* has increased with the growth of *branding*: that is, production of goods carrying manufacturers' trademarks. An independent wholesaler may not promote the sale of a branded article as strongly as the manufacturer would like. Consequently some manufacturers set up selling departments to do the work of wholesaling. Their aim is to ensure that as many retailers as possible stock their brands. The manufacturer retains the profit usually made by the wholesaler but against this benefit must be set the extra distribution costs incurred by the selling department.

Another method of distribution is *direct selling* from the manufacturer to the consumer. Thus the maker undertakes the work of wholesaling and retailing in addition to manufacturing. Some makers of commodities such as cleaning materials, cosmetics, etc, take their goods straight to the homes of consumers. These goods are usually those in steady demand throughout the year. Other manufacturers open their own retail shops to sell goods such as shoes and clothing, or set up mail-order departments.

Direct selling to consumers has a number of benefits. In the first place, the maker is assured that sales representatives sell only the maker's products and not other makes – an assurance which cannot be given when sales are made to independent retailers. Secondly, by having close contact with consumers the maker is able to note any changes in demand quickly and to investigate the cause. In addition, consumers' complaints can be dealt with promptly. Thirdly, the manufacturer retains the profits usually made by the wholesaler and the retailer.

On the other hand, when the wholesaler and retailer are by-passed, the manufacturer has to undertake the functions of both, thereby incurring the expense and trouble that this involves.

Thus conditions vary in different trades. The main motive for direct selling is the maker's wish to maximise sales effort. Against the benefits of direct selling must be balanced the extra distribution costs involved. As a result of the latter, many makers prefer to deal with wholesalers who will perform the functions outlined in Section 5.1.

6.3   Agricultural Commodities

Agricultural producers face problems which are not encountered by the makers of manufactured goods.

1 The manufacturer can regulate output in response to demand.

A farmer, however, cannot increase output quickly if demand increases. The period from seed-time to harvest may be many months, while the rearing of animals may take several years. Consequently farm production cannot be changed quickly, as factory production can. Further, the crop may be abundant or poor according to weather conditions and other factors outside the producer's control.

2 The manufacturer can standardise products so that each unit of output is virtually identical. Cars, washing-machines and vacuum-cleaners are examples of standardised articles. The farmer, on the other hand, has little control over the quantity, quality and size of some crops. In order to ensure certain qualities or sizes, farm products (such as wheat, tomatoes and eggs) must be selected and graded.

3 Most factory goods can be stored easily in warehouses. Those that have a seasonal demand, such as fireworks or Christmas trade goods, can be produced steadily throughout the year and stored until they are needed. On the other hand, many farm products are highly perishable and have to be marketed in as short a time and with as little handling as possible. Consequently the output and prices of farm products vary more than those of manufactured goods.

As a result of the difficulties outlined above, the channels of distribution for agricultural products are relatively complicated. However, the main methods are discussed below.

Sales direct to consumers

Some producers sell from roadside stalls, or undertake house-to-house sales of such items as vegetables and milk. Commodities such as butter and eggs may be sold from stalls at local markets.

Sales direct to retailers

Dairy produce, poultry, vegetables, etc. may be sold direct to retailers.

Sales to wholesalers

The production of many fresh foods is undertaken by a large number of small producers who are often situated in remote areas. Consequently they sell very little locally to either consumers or retailers. In such cases, it is usual for *wholesale merchants* to buy from them and arrange for the goods to be sold at large wholesale markets. Alternatively, *commission salespeople* are employed by farmers to sell their produce. These salespeople undertake to find buyers and charge a commission for their services. Together with wholesale merchants, commission salespeople form the principal sellers at large wholesale markets. Most large towns have wholesale agricultural produce markets like that at Covent Garden. A central market allows buyers to see and choose the goods required. Inspection is a necessity when perishable goods are dealt in, because buyers want to make certain that their purchases are fresh.

At those markets the principal buyers are: *local retailers* who make their purchases and take the goods away with them in their own transport, and *wholesale merchants* who require supplies to send to wholesalers and retailers serving outlying districts.

Sales to manufacturers

Some producers agree to grow crops of vegetables and fruit for manufacturers who buy the entire crop and process it. These products – tinned, frozen or bottled by the manufacturer – are then distributed in the same way as manufactured goods.

Sales through marketing boards

Marketing boards have been in existence for many years. They serve to prevent violent fluctuations in the income of agricultural producers. Farming is a very uncertain business. Incomes may be high in some years but low in others. A good harvest, for example, may result in low prices (and hence, low incomes for producers) particularly if the crop is perishable and has to be marketed in as short a time as possible. The boards seek to achieve their purpose by *regulating the supply* of commodities.

A marketing board is a *statutory monopoly* and controls the producers of the commodity with which it is concerned. Thus, with certain exceptions, it is compulsory for all producers wishing to sell a commodity covered by a marketing scheme to *register* with the board concerned and to abide by its directions and regulations. For instance, marketing boards exist for milk, hops, wool and potatoes. The producers elect members to the board and these members are responsible for carrying out the marketing scheme. The expenses of the scheme are met by dues paid by producers who work under the board's arrangements.

A board may buy up all supplies of the product and act as a *selling agency* on a national basis. Alternatively, it may maintain a broad control over marketing conditions but leave producers free to sell their own produce. Thus a board may influence total output by determining the acreage to be planted by each producer. Again, it may fix the prices and terms of sale. When supplies are plentiful a board may enter the market and buy surplus stocks in order to prevent prices from falling.

Many thousands of small-scale producers are able to take advantage of the distributive organisation established by the marketing boards. The producers have an assured market and know beforehand how much will be received for a particular crop.

6.4 Raw Materials

Industry requires supplies of raw materials to use in manufacturing. Although some raw materials such as coal are produced in Britain, most raw materials have to be imported from countries abroad.

Organised markets called *commodity exchanges* or *produce exchanges* provide meeting places where importers sell raw materials to wholesalers. Examples are the Wool Exchange, the Metal Exchange and the London Commodity Exchange in the City of London. Often an exchange is sited near the docks where the commodity is warehoused. Business is carried on according to a definite set of rules, although the actual procedure depends on whether the commodity is capable of being *graded*. Where grading is possible, as with wheat and cotton, the commodity need not actually be on view in the market. However, some commodities, such as wool and tea, vary in quality, and an opportunity must be given to buyers to inspect samples before the sale.

Commodity markets are conducted by *brokers* who act as agents for buyers and sellers. Commodities which can be easily graded are sold by *private treaty*; those which cannot be accurately graded and have, therefore, to be sampled and tested, are sold by *auction*.

Raw wool cannot easily be graded because there is great variation in the quality of the wool even in different parts of the same fleece. Upon its arrival in this country the importer instructs brokers to sort and classify the wool in the warehouses, to prepare catalogues, send them to potential buyers and arrange for the wool to be auctioned on the Wool Exchange.

Buying brokers visit the warehouse to sample the wool and make notes on its quality in their catalogues. This information assists them in their bidding at the auction.

The auctions occur in six series of wool sales in a year, each series lasting about three weeks. In the auction room the buying brokers sit at desks arranged in semicircular tiers facing the selling brokers. The selling brokers occupy the rostrum in turn and offer the wool, lot by lot, on behalf of their clients. The various lots are sold to the highest bidders.

After each sale, the selling broker sends a *sold contract note* to the buyer, stating the full particulars of the wool purchased. Later an *invoice* is sent to the buyer, showing the date of payment.

To the producer of the wool, the broker sends an *account of sales* showing the price obtained, the commission and charges, and the date of which payment will be made. In due course the broker remits the net proceeds to the grower by paying the sum due into the London office of the producer's bank.

In contrast to wool, many imported commodities are disposed of by private sales (private treaty) through brokers who maintain contacts with buyers. A common form of procedure is for the importer to notify a broker when a consignment is available for sale. The broker then obtains offers from potential buyers and submits the prices to the importer. Some bargaining may take place, after which the broker will arrange a *contract* for the importer and also arrange delivery of the consignment to the purchaser.

Thus, brokers in the commodity markets perform a number of useful functions. They bring buyers and sellers together and often they arrange delivery of the commodity to the buyer. In addition, brokers maintain contacts with buyers and sellers so that their advice is useful to producers and others who seek infor- mation on market movements. The charges made by brokers are relatively small, and are generally considered to be much less than the cost to the producers of marketing their produce themselves.

Transactions on an exchange may be either for immediate (*spot*) *delivery* or *future delivery* at one, two or three months ahead. In this way the seller is guaranteed a sale, while the buyer is sure of future supplies of raw materials. Generally, only commodities which can be graded into standardised qualities can be bought and sold by means of *forward contracts*. Such commodities can be bought or sold without being seen because buyers and sellers know exactly what the grades mean.

Futures and hedging

Forward contracts are also known as *futures* and dealings in futures take place in such raw materials as cocoa, coffee, sugar and rubber.

In a *futures market* there are people called *speculators* who are keenly interested in changes in prices and who try to take advantage of price fluctuations in order to make a profit for themselves. Speculators rarely buy or sell the actual commodity, but instead buy or sell *futures contracts*. The existence of such speculators makes it possible for manufacturers and importers who store commodities, to 'insure' against risks of loss caused by changes in price. For example, if importers who hold commodities for long periods fear a future fall in price, they can sell futures now to a speculator and so assure themselves of receiving the present price. By so doing they insure against loss caused by a fall in price. On the other hand, the buyer of the futures is speculating against such a fall in price, and hopes to be able to sell at a higher price at the agreed date.

In a similar way, if a coffee manufacturer thinks the spot price of coffee is likely to rise in the next few months, futures may be bought (if they are quoted at a lower price than is expected to prevail in the future) as a *hedge* against a rise in the price. If in fact the spot price rises higher than the price of the futures contract, the manufacturer receives the difference between the spot price and the price of the futures contract. Thus there is compensation for the *loss* on the raw material due to its rise in price by the *gain* on the futures contract. Alternatively, if the price of coffee falls, the manufacturer buys on the spot market and pays the difference to the seller of the futures. Thus the loss on the futures contract, due to not accepting delivery, is offset by the gain on the raw material due to its fall in price.

Functions of commodity exchanges

Commodity exchanges serve the following purposes:

- they facilitate the marketing of raw materials by provision of a central meeting-place for the convenience of buyers and sellers;
- they enable buyers to ensure future supplies of raw materials;
- they enable producers to sell crops in advance at an assured price;

- they enable buyers to cover themselves against fluctuations in price by hedging (this function applies only when graded commodities make a futures market possible).

Test Yourself

1 Define the term 'market'.
2 Give two examples of markets which have particular locations.
3 Give two examples of worldwide markets.
4 Briefly describe the market for consumer goods.
5 Give three examples of producers' goods.
6 List the principal ways in which manufactured goods are distributed to customers.
7 What are (a) the benefits and (b) the drawbacks of selling direct to consumers?
8 What is the main motive for selling direct to consumers?
9 List the special problems faced by farmers.
10 What are the main channels of distribution for agricultural products?
11 What is the purpose of marketing boards?
12 What determines whether a commodity is sold (a) by private treaty, or (b) by auction?
13 What does 'spot' delivery mean?
14 What is a speculator?
15 How does speculation assist traders in commodities?
16 Define 'hedging'.
17 Briefly describe the work of brokers on the Wool Exchange.
18 What are the functions of commodity exchanges?

Chapter 7

Consumers

Consumers buy goods and services for the purpose of satisfying wants. Many purchases are made for cash, but very often a shopper can choose between prompt cash payment or postponing payment until later. Buying now and paying later is called *buying on credit*. Organisations which operate credit facilities have to obtain a licence from the *Office of Fair Trading* (see page 79), which has power to refuse or take away licences, if necessary.

The principal ways of obtaining credit are:

- hire purchase
- credit sale
- shop budget account
- trading checks
- mail-order credit
- credit cards.

The cost of credit

In most cases buying on credit costs money. The exception is 'interest-free credit' where the cash price is simply divided into a number of payments spread over a period with no extra charges for credit. However, for other loans on which interest is payable the cost of credit is the Annual Percentage Rate (APR) of charge. This is a measurement of the total cost for credit expressed as an annual rate. It includes interest on the loan itself and any other charges payable as a condition of getting the loan, e.g. maintenance charges for a television set on hire purchase, or administration costs.

Most advertisements containing detailed information about credit have to show the APR. Thus consumers can compare one credit scheme with another.

7.1   Forms of Instalment Credit

Hire purchase

Hire purchase is a very neat description. A customer hires the goods until payment is completed. Only then has the customer purchased the goods and become the owner.

When goods are bought on hire purchase, a *deposit* has to be paid, and the remainder of the price plus hire purchase charges are divided into equal weekly or monthly *instalments* payable over a fixed period. The period of time depends on government regulations.

The customer is given a *hire purchase agreement* to sign. The agreement forms a contract between the customer and the shop (or *finance company*, if one is involved). The shop or finance company undertakes to hire out the goods at a fixed rental and for a fixed period. At the end of this time the customer has the option of becoming the legal owner by buying the goods for a nominal sum (such as £1) or simply by paying the last instalment.

Kinds of goods
Goods particularly suitable for hire purchase trading are:

* the more expensive goods which have a long life – to last at least as long as they are being paid for;
* those which have a good resale value.

Examples of these kinds of goods are cars and furniture.

Finance companies
A hire purchase agreement may be with the retailer who sells the goods, or with a finance company. A small retail business may be unable to afford to sell, for example, cars on hire purchase and the agreement will be made with a finance company. In these circumstances when a customer buys goods, they are in fact sold to the finance company. The retailer receives the cash price from the company and the latter makes an agreement with the customer for the hire of the goods.

Hire purchase charges
These charges consist of *interest* together with certain *costs*, such as collection and office expenses.

Legal protection
Special protection is given to the customer by law in hire purchase transactions if the cost of the goods plus hire purchase

charges is £15 000 or less. The customer has three important rights:

- the right to information
- the right to withdraw
- protection against repossession.

Information   Before an agreement is signed, a customer must be given the cash price of the goods in writing. This figure can be compared with the hire purchase price of the goods to see how much extra has to be paid. (Hire purchase price is the amount of deposit plus the total of the instalments.)

A customer must be given a copy of the signed agreement which contains a description of the goods, their cash price and hire purchase price, the amount of each instalment and the date instalments are due.

Right to Withdraw   If the agreement is signed either at a customer's home, or at a place other than *appropriate trade premises* (which are for instance, a shop, showroom or finance company office) the customer has five days in which to cancel it.

There is no 'cooling off' period if an agreement is signed on trade premises. It is assumed that a customer who goes there has had a chance to think over the matter.

A customer who does not wish to keep up the instalments for some reason can hand the goods back voluntarily at any time. However, if this happens, the instalments will have to be paid up to the date of return. If they come to less than half the hire purchase price, the customer must make up the difference unless a County Court Judge lays down a lesser sum.

Protection against Repossession   The law provides a certain amount of protection to those who fall behind with their hire purchase payments. If less than one third of the hire purchase price has been paid the owner is entitled to come and take away the goods. After one-third of the hire purchase price has been paid, the goods cannot be taken away unless the customer ends the agreement or unless the owner gets a court order. One of the courses open to the court in these circumstances is to make an order laying down the terms on which the customer shall pay the amount due and to allow the goods to be kept if payment is made. This may be very helpful in giving a second chance to someone who has run into financial difficulties.

An example of hire purchase

The *cash price* of a motor-cycle is £312. If buying on hire purchase, the customer pays a deposit of £105 and then either

£3.30 a week over 18 months (in which case the *hire purchase price* is £362.40) or £2.70 a week over 2 years (in which case the hire purchase price is £385.80).

If the customer decides to spread payments over 18 months, the extra cost of hire purchase is £50.40 which works out at a charge of approximately 24% per year. Over the 2-year period the additional cost is £73.80 which is approximately 36% per year.

Advantages of hire purchase to the buyer

● This is one of the most convenient ways of buying on credit. Almost anyone – provided they have a steady job and a clear record as a borrower – can get goods on hire purchase.
● Goods can be obtained when they are needed most instead of the buyer having to do without them until the cash price has been saved. A newly married couple, for example, would need a lot of money to furnish a home all at once.
● The customer may be able to buy an article of better quality than would be possible if the full cash price had to be found immediately.
● By making payments out of income, a customer may be able to keep money savings available to meet any unforeseen contingency.
● The alternative of saving up over a lengthy period in order to pay cash presents difficulties for some people, whereas they may find it easier to manage a regular commitment.
● By the time the necessary cash has been saved, the price of the goods may well have risen.

Disadvantages of hire purchase to the buyer

● A customer can buy only those goods which have a resale value, and the method is unsuitable for small purchases.
● A customer has no right to sell the goods until the final instalment has been paid.
● Hire purchase can be one of the more expensive ways of borrowing.
● Some sellers do not offer hire purchase terms, so a hirer wishing to make use of instalment credit may be restricted as to choice of retail outlets.
● A hirer who fails to maintain repayments is likely to lose both the article and the money paid for hiring it.

Advantages of hire purchase to the seller

- By offering facilities for payment by instalments a seller attracts additional customers, namely those who cannot pay the full cash price immediately. Thus total sales are increased.
- The increased turnover creates a faster rate of stockturn. The benefits of increasing the rate of turnover are outlined on page 122.
- The article out on hire acts as security for the hirer's debt. If the hire purchase agreement is broken the seller can reclaim the article.
- The seller receives a relatively high rate of interest on the money owed. If the agreement is financed by a finance company then the seller receives a commission on each sale.

Disadvantages of hire purchase to the seller

- Although the article serves as security for the amount owing, it may, if reclaimed, have been so damaged or poorly maintained as to be virtually worthless.
- The seller incurs clerical costs since records must be kept of amounts owing, payments made, etc.
- A trader who offers instalment credit requires a larger capital than the trader who sells for cash only. This requirement can be avoided, however, by using the services of a finance company.

Credit sale

Some shops offer the choice of obtaining goods on *credit sale* or *hire purchase*. The difference is legal rather than financial.

- When goods are bought on hire purchase, the goods are hired until the final instalment is paid, but with a credit sale the goods are owned as soon as the agreement is made.
- If a customer falls behind with instalments, the goods cannot be taken away as they can in hire purchase. The seller can, however, sue the customer for debt.
- Under a credit sale agreement, the customer has no right to end the agreement and hand the goods back.
- A hirer cannot sell the goods until all instalments have been paid. The buyer may sell the goods but all instalments owing must be paid off.

Legal protection
The transaction is protected by the Consumer Credit Act if:

- the purchase is over £50 and not more than £15 000;
- payment is to be made in five or more instalments.

In these circumstances a document known as a *credit sale agreement* is compulsory.

A customer who signs a credit sale agreement covered by the Consumer Credit Act has two important rights:

- the right to *information* – as for hire purchase;
- the right to *withdraw* (if the agreement is signed at a customer's home or any other place except 'trade premises' the customer has at least five days in which to cancel the agreement).

An example of credit sale
The cash price of a record player is £63. If it is bought under a credit sale agreement, the customer does not pay a deposit but makes 38 weekly payments of £1.95. The total credit price is £74.10. The customer is paying, therefore, an extra £11.10 which is a charge of approximately 18%.

Kinds of goods
A customer is not restricted to buying goods which have a resale value. There are some goods which are more suitable for selling by credit sale. For example, hand-tailored clothes are made to fit a particular person and cannot be taken back (as they would have to be if they were the subject of a hire purchase agreement) for resale.

Whether a customer is offered hire purchase or credit sale, or both, depends on the policy of the shop or finance company.

Advantages of credit sale to the buyer

- The goods belong to the buyer from the start.
- They cannot be taken back if a buyer falls behind with the instalments (as can happen if goods are bought on a hire purchase agreement).
- Hire purchase regulations about minimum cash deposits do not apply if repayment is within nine months.

Disadvantages of credit sale to the buyer

- A buyer lacks protection from the Consumer Credit Act if the cash value of the goods is £50 or less.

- Goods cannot be handed back if the buyer wishes to cancel the agreement.

Like hire purchase, a credit sale is a fairly expensive way of borrowing money, but there are few formalities and it enables buyers to obtain immediate use of goods and pay for them out of future earnings.

Under a credit sale agreement the seller has the trouble of suing the buyer if instalments are not paid.

Shop budget accounts

A budget or *subscription account* at a store offers buyers the opportunity to borrow continuously up to a certain sum.

A typical budget account works as follows. The customer agrees to pay a certain sum every month to the store, which allows credit to the value of, say, ten times that payment. For example, a customer makes a cash payment of £6 and receives credit for $10 \times £6 = £60$. Up to £60 can then be spent in the shop. As each monthly payment is paid into the account, further purchases can be made provided the debt does not go beyond the £60 limit.

Some shops give *revolving credit*, as it is sometimes called, only up to six times the amount paid into the budget account. Others give as much as twenty-four times the amount.

Cost of a budget account

Shops make a *service charge* for revolving credit. Some may charge a small sum in the pound on the monthly balance while other stores charge a certain sum (£0.05 is a common figure) on each payment made into the account.

Advantages of a budget account

The major advantage of a budget account lies in its convenience. A customer can do shopping without paying cash and without having to sign hire purchase or credit sale agreements. Each month the store sends a statement showing details of purchases made.

Disadvantages of budget accounts

- A customer's choice of goods is restricted either to a single shop or to a group of shops.
- The actual rate of interest over a year works out at a good deal more than 'the small service charge' of 5% quoted by many

shops. Typical rates of interest are between 8 and 20%. Hence, it is a costly way of borrowing.

Trading checks

There are over 400 check trading companies and they all operate on approximately the same system. Credit is offered in the form of trading checks or *vouchers*. The amount of credit is commonly up to £100 but sometimes up to about £500.

Checks can be used to buy goods in shops listed in a booklet provided for customers by the check trading company. The number of shops varies. The largest companies have many thousands of shops listed while the smaller local companies may authorise only a few dozen.

When a customer buys goods, the value of the purchases is written on the customer's check. The customer pays nothing and the check trading company pays the shop for the goods.

Repayment
The check trading company collects from customers by instalments. Usually an *agent* will call on customers once a week. Amounts up to £30 have to be repaid over 20 weeks. Larger amounts can be repaid over periods of up to about two years.

Cost
For a £20 check a customer may pay £1 followed by 20 weekly instalments of £1 each. In this case, therefore, the service charge is £1 or around 25% a year.

Advantages of trading checks

- A customer can borrow the full price of goods, whereas with hire purchase or credit sale, it may be necessary to put down a deposit.
- Trading checks enable shoppers to buy what they want when needed, without waiting or dipping into savings.

Disadvantages of trading checks

- Customers are limited to stores on the check company's list.
- Prices in these shops may be higher than in shops selling for cash only, because they have to pay the check company for directing trade to them.

Mail-order credit

Credit is available from the large mail-order firms which rely on catalogues of goods for sale sent out to attract their customers. Most work through agents who obtain business from neighbours and friends. Customers may spread payment for purchases over a number of weeks. Catalogue prices may be higher than those in some shops, but the savings in fares from shopping at home may make it worthwhile to pay the dearer catalogue price.

Credit cards

A credit card such as Access, Barclaycard or Trustcard enables the holder to pay for many goods or services by producing the card. Each cardholder has a borrowing limit and a monthly statement shows how much money is outstanding. The credit card company allows approximately 25 days to settle the bill, charging no interest if payment is made in full.

A cardholder who plans spending carefully and makes repayments on time, has the convenience of shopping without cash and the advantage of full use of the bank's credit facilities.

Many large store groups, including supermarket chains, operate their own credit cards. These *shop credit cards* work in various ways. They can, for instance, be used with budget accounts (see page 71). Another type of scheme works like an ordinary credit card. Either the amount owing can be settled in full each month or a part only of the debt is paid. Interest is charged on the balance outstanding each month. Shop credit cards are useful when a number of purchases are made at one shop, but choice is limited.

Hire purchase, credit sale, budget accounts, trading checks, mail-order and credit cards provide various means by which customers can buy goods and pay for them later.

Buying goods on credit means borrowing money from the shopkeeper or finance company in order to have goods now and make payment later. An alternative method of financing purchases is to borrow money and pay the full cash price immediately.

7.2 Loans

There are a number of ways of raising money in order to pay for goods in full at the time of purchase.

Borrowing from banks

A person with a bank account may be able to borrow from the bank either by having an *overdraft* or by getting an *ordinary loan* or a *personal loan*. If the bank manager grants an overdraft of £200, this means that cheques can be written until the customer owes the bank £200. The whole amount has to be repaid by a fixed date or by instalments. With an ordinary loan the customer borrows all the loan at once and repays in agreed instalments with interest. Banks also operate a personal loan scheme. A borrower takes the full amount at the start and pays back by regular instalments. The differences from an ordinary loan lie in the method of charging interest and the security required.

Cost
On overdrafts, interest is charged only on the amount out-standing on a day-to-day basis, and not on the whole loan.

On ordinary loans the customer is charged at the current rate of interest throughout the period of the loan. Interest is at a slightly higher rate than that charged on an overdraft.

The interest rate on personal loans is higher than the rates charged on overdrafts and ordinary loans. However, it is a fixed rate, whereas on an overdraft or an ordinary loan the interest may vary during the period of the borrowing.

Security required
For overdrafts and ordinary loans, the bank may ask for *security* to cover the loan. The advantage of a personal loan is that no security is needed to cover the loan, but *references* will be required.

Length of loan
Banks prefer to lend for short periods: namely from a few weeks to a year or so. On occasion they may lend over a longer period of up to ten years if a customer agrees to make regular repayments.

Advantages of bank loans

- Banks provide the cheapest method of borrowing.

- With an overdraft, the borrower does not start paying interest until money is actually owed to the bank.
- Personal loans give those who have no security to offer a method of borrowing which is an alternative to that provided by hire purchase or credit sale.

Disadvantages of bank loans

- Only bank customers can get an overdraft or an ordinary loan (but anyone can apply to a bank for a personal loan.)
- A bank reserves the right to withdraw overdraft facilities at any time. In practice, it seldom does so.

Life assurance policy loans

Holders of either *whole life* or *endowment assurance policies* (see Section 16.3) are usually entitled to borrow money from the insurance company once their policies have acquired surrender value.

The *surrender value* is the cash sum that the company would pay the holder if the policy was given up. In the early years of a policy, the surrender value tends to be low and in the first two or three years it may be nothing at all. Consequently the longer a policy is held, the higher becomes the surrender value.

The insurance company will usually lend up to 90% of the surrender value. Interest rates vary between companies but usually they are as favourable as rates charged by banks.

The policy is held by the company during the period of the loan. The sum borrowed need not be repaid until the policy matures. Borrowing on a life assurance policy is an easy way of raising money, but it is limited to policies which have been in existence long enough to have acquired a cash surrender value.

Finance companies

Finance companies lend money to *traders* to finance hire purchase and credit sale transactions. They also make *personal loans* to individuals to finance certain projects such as central heating installation, the building of a garage or the purchase of a car.

Finance company personal loans are often arranged through garages, shops, etc. Alternatively a person wishing to borrow may approach a finance company directly. No security is required.

Usually, the finance company settles the builder's or contractor's account directly and the borrower repays the finance company in monthly instalments over a period of up to ten years. Rates of interest are generally the same as for hire purchase.

Advantage
Finance company personal loans are usually easier to obtain than bank loans if there is a *credit squeeze*.

Disadvantages

- Generally, these loans are available only for a limited range of expensive purchases.
- Like hire purchase, this can be a costly way of borrowing.

Building societies

Few people have enough money to buy a home for cash. The others have to borrow most of the money needed and this is usually done by getting a *mortgage*. This is a loan against the security of the property purchased. The borrower pays back the cost in equal monthly payments. If the repayments are not kept up, the lender can sell the property and get the loan back.

Applications for loans for *house purchase* may be made to a bank, an insurance company, a local authority or a building society – but the latter are the principal source of loans and exist for the purpose. Usually societies will lend up to 80% of the house's value, but sometimes a society will advance up to 100%. The loan is limited to 2½ to 3 times the borrower's annual income. The money is repayable in instalments over a period of years, the time allowed depending on the society and the borrower's age. Sometimes societies allow up to 35 years.

Credit unions

These are small savings and loans clubs where members agree to pool part of their savings in order to provide themselves with low cost credit. The Credit Unions Act 1979 requires that members of a credit union should have a 'common bond' such as living in the same street or housing estate, attending the same church or social club, or working at the same firm. Regular savings provide a fund of money from which amounts may be borrowed if and when a need arises. Thus a credit union is, in effect, a *savings and loans club*.

7.3 Leasing

An alternative to buying goods is to lease them. This means hiring items in return for an annual rental for the agreed period of the contract. Leasing is attractive to businesses because it permits the use of land, buildings or equipment without spending large sums of money on purchasing. In addition, it enables the latest equipment to be acquired with each renewal of the lease. Consumers may arrange to lease goods such as cars, television sets, video recorders, etc.

7.4 Consumer Protection

Protection for shoppers against dangerous or poor quality goods is provided by legislation, by the government, by various independent organisations and by industry and trade.

Laws that protect the consumer

The most important of these laws are outlined below.

Weights and Measures Acts (1963 to 1979)
These protect consumers against shortages in both weight and measure of goods.

The Food and Drugs Act (1955 and 1976)
This lays down a *code* covering the composition and purity of foods sold by retailers. There are also certain controls regarding the labelling and description of foods.

The Trade Descriptions Act (1968 and 1972)
This ensures as far as possible that people tell the truth about goods, prices, and services. Thus the quantity, size and composition of goods must be correctly stated by traders. In addition a statement concerning the date of manufacture must be true. As well as written descriptions, the Act covers oral statements made by a trader.

The Consumer Protection Act (1987)
This provides for the adoption of *safety regulations*. From time to time a safety regulation has been imposed on many goods including oil heaters, gas and electric fire guards, cooking utensils and toys.

The Sale of Goods Act (1979)

This makes a *retailer* responsible for ensuring that goods sold are fit for the purpose for which such goods are normally used, and that they meet the description applied to them. If they are not fit for their purpose the buyer is entitled to return them and claim a refund. Thus if a new bucket leaks the buyer is entitled to return it. The same applies if, for example, a blanket described as blue turns out to be pink. In this respect, a customer's rights cannot be taken away by any *guarantee* signed; and guarantees do not take away a *manufacturer's liability* for damages or loss resulting from a defect in a product caused by the manufacturer's neglect. Minimum standards for the supply of *services*, e.g. car repairs or decorating, are laid down by *The Supply of Goods and Services Act (1982)*.

The Fair Trading Act (1973)

This established the Office of Fair Trading to watch over the effect upon consumers' interests of trading practices and commercial activities, and to recommend government action where necessary.

The Prices Act (1974)

This requires retailers to mark *unit prices* on certain goods. For example, the price ticket on a bag of potatoes has to show price per pound or kilogram as well as the price of that particular bag. Unit pricing helps shoppers to make direct comparison of price and quantity. Date marking of foodstuffs is also compulsory under this Act.

The Consumer Credit Act (1974)

This ensures that people are given information about their credit or hire transactions, including the true annual percentage rate of interest charged. *Truth in lending* is the main aim of the Act.

The Financial Services Act (1986)

Investors are protected by this Act. A Securities and Investments Board (SIB) was established to oversee the operation of all financial services businesses. In order to carry out investment business, a firm must be authorised by the SIB. The latter delegates this task to self-regulatory organisations (SROs), each of which oversees a specific field of investment. Examples include the Securities Association; the Financial Intermediaries, Managers and Brokers Regulatory Association (FIMBRA); and the Life Assurance and Unit Trust Regulatory Association (LAUTRO).

Many of these laws are enforced by *local authorities*; a consumer, for example, who considers a retailer has deliberately given short measure can report the matter to the *trading standards* or *consumer protection department* of the local authority. Similarly, food purchased which proves unfit for consumption can be reported to the *environmental health department*.

The government and the consumer

Matters concerning consumers are the concern of various government departments and the nationalised industries.

Government departments
The main function of government departments is to administer the powers given to them by Acts of Parliament.

- *The Department of Trade and Industry* is the department chiefly responsible for matters affecting most consumer goods and services. For example it has overall responsibility for weights and measures law. Inspectors employed by local authorities (but who qualify through examination by the Department of Trade and Industry) regularly check the accuracy of weights, measures and scales and of measuring instruments such as petrol pumps. Traders whose equipment is at fault are liable to prosecution. The Department is also responsible for consumer protection and consumer credit. Other legislation administered by the Department includes the Trade Descriptions Act and the Consumer Credit Act.
- *The Ministry of Agriculture, Fisheries and Food* is responsible for regulations governing the supply and manufacture of food, its labelling and advertising. Other functions include the regulation of slaughterhouses and the quality of milk.
- *The Department of Health and Social Security* shares with the Ministry of Agriculture responsibility under the Food and Drugs Act 1955. It is concerned with food hygiene, and with the provisions of the Act which apply to medicinal products.
- *The Home Office* is responsible for some aspects of *public safety*, such as the control of explosives, firearms and dangerous drugs.

The Office of Fair Trading is a government agency, headed by the *Director General of Fair Trading*, which helps consumers in a number of ways. For example, information is published to assist people to know their rights and where they can go for help; new laws can be proposed to end unfair trading methods; and legal action can be taken against traders who persistently break their obligations to consumers. The Office does not deal with individual complaints: these are dealt with locally by trading standards departments, citizens' advice bureaux or consumer advice centres.

The National Consumer Council, set up by the government in 1975, represents consumers' views to the government, to the Director General of Fair Trading, and to industry. It deals with legislation, advertising standards and methods, the service given by consumer advice centres, and facilities for testing products. It is financed by the government and its chairman and members are appointed by the Secretary of State for Trade and Industry.

Nationalised industries

Under legislation governing nationalised industries, there is provision for *consumers' councils* which consider matters relating to consumers' satisfaction. For example, if an enquiry has not been properly dealt with at an electricity showroom, and satisfaction cannot be obtained by writing to the district office manager, then the matter may be referred to the consultative council. (Each electricity board has a consumer council.) Besides enquiring into consumer complaints, a council advises its board on issues that may effect the consumer.

Independent organisations

There are a number of independent bodies which provide help in the field of consumer problems and in so doing make an important contribution to consumer protection.

Consumers' Association

The Consumers' Association is a non-profit-making association which seeks to improve the quality of goods and services available to shoppers. It does so by comparative testing, the results of which are made available in its magazine *Which?*

The Association is financed by subscriptions from members and the sale of its publications. Members receive a copy of *Which?* every month.

A feature of *Which?* reports is the choice of a *best buy* from products tested, except when it is considered that no product can be selected as offering the best 'value for money'.

British Standards Institution

The British Standards Institution is concerned with standards for consumer goods. A *standard* is a technical document which lays down the level of performance or safety a product must meet, or sometimes the dimensions to which it must be made to ensure a precise fit – as with plugs and sockets. On a car seat-belt, for example, the standard would specify what the breaking strain must be, what force the buckle must withstand before it flies open under impact and so on. If a manufacturer's product conforms to British Standard specifications it can be awarded the *kite-mark* which is the BSI's seal of approval. The range of products which have been awarded the kite-mark includes electric blankets, oil heaters, pressure cookers and many others.

A firm wishing to show the kite-mark must allow the Institution to choose samples of the product for testing. British Standards Institution inspectors visit factories to ensure that quality is maintained after the kite-mark has been granted.

Fig. 7.1 *Labels which help the consumer*

BSI kite-mark

British Electrotechnical Approvals Board
Mark of Approval

Citizens' Advice Bureaux

Citizens' Advice Bureaux are established in most large towns. They are centres of free information and advice, given in confidence to any person on any question he or she cares to ask. There are upwards of 600 bureaux in Great Britain and Northern Ireland. Each year they handle a great number of inquiries on a wide variety of subjects including complaints from consumers.

Local consumer groups

These groups investigate goods and services in local areas and publish their findings in a bulletin. Most groups restrict their activities to collecting and classifying useful information: they might, for example, compile a list of local tradespeople who do a reliable job at a fair price.

Consumer advice centres
The aim of these centres is to give pre-shopping information and advice. They deal also with shoppers' complaints about faulty goods and services. The centres are organised and financed by local councils.

Industry and trade organisations

Several organisations have been set up for the advising of consumers. Some of the better known organisations are listed below.

Retail Trading Standards Association
Many shops, especially department stores, belong to the RTSA which runs a testing laboratory where complaints from shoppers about textiles can be investigated. The Association is concerned with the good name of its members and brings influence to bear on those who attempt to mislead or cheat the public.

The British Electrotechnical Approvals Board for Domestic Appliances
BEAB tests and approves domestic electrical appliances for safety. The BEAB Mark of Approval (on page 81) is near the rating plate and identifies every appliance which has been approved for safety. Non-domestic electrical appliances, such as light fittings, power tools and table fans (which are approved for electrical safety by the British Standards Institution) carry the BSI kite-mark illustrated on page 81.

British Gas
British Gas has a research and testing centre and operates an approval scheme for domestic gas appliances. No appliance can be put on sale in a gas showroom unless it is approved by British Gas.

Trade associations

These are bodies formed by traders in the same line of business. Although trade associations exist primarily to protect the interests of their members, they are increasingly conscious of customers' views. Some associations have *codes of practice* which guide members on how to look after customers. The codes also state how complaints should be handled. Thus travel agents who are members of the Association of British Travel Agents (ABTA) agree to follow the standards of conduct set out in the Association's code of practice. ABTA also operates a compensation fund to safeguard customers who have reserved holidays with a member firm which defaults. Similarly, members of the Mail Order Traders' Association must operate according to certain rules.

Test Yourself

1 Why does a seller charge interest when selling on credit?
2 When does a buyer of goods on hire purchase actually become the owner?
3 Which types of goods are most suitable for hire purchase trading?
4 Briefly explain the part played by a finance company in hire purchase trading.
5 Name three important rights provided by law for buyers on hire purchase.
6 What are some disadvantages to the buyer of using hire purchase as a method of purchasing?
7 Write down three ways in which a credit sale agreement differs from hire purchase.
8 Name three advantages to the buyer of using a credit sale agreement.
9 Briefly describe how 'revolving credit' works.
10 Briefly describe how a consumer can obtain credit by means of trading checks.
11 Why is mail-order credit attractive to consumers?
12 What are the advantages of credit cards to consumers?
13 Name the two chief ways a bank will lend to customers.
14 When can a life assurance policy be used to borrow money?
15 What is a mortgage?
16 State briefly how a credit union operates.
17 What is leasing?
18 What are the advantages of leasing?
19 What is the purpose of the Trade Descriptions Acts (1968 and 1972)?
20 How does the Sale of Goods Act (1979) assist consumers?
21 Name the Act which provides minimum standards for the supply of services.
22 What is the job of the Director General of Fair Trading?
23 Which Act requires retailers to mark unit prices?

24 Who enforces laws protecting the consumer?
25 How do government departments provide consumer protection?
26 Which government department is chiefly responsible for questions about consumer goods and services?
27 Which department is concerned with the safety aspects of consumer protection?
28 Which body represents consumers' views to the government and to industry?
29 Name the consumer protection service provided by a nationalised industry.
30 Name the organisation that publishes the magazine *Which?*
31 Name the seal of approval issued by the British Standards Institution.
32 Name the kind of goods which are the major concern of the Retail Trading Standards Association.
33 What does BEAB stand for?
34 What is a trade association?

Chapter 8

Private Enterprise

Goods and services are provided by undertakings which are either privately or publicly owned. Publicly owned undertakings are operated by the state or by local authorities.

In this chapter the various forms of private ownership are described. They include the sole proprietor, partnership, joint-stock company and the co-operative society. Each form of organisation has particular characteristics of ownership, control, raising of capital and disposal of profits.

8.1 Sole Proprietors

The trader in business on his or her own is known as a *sole trader* or *proprietor*. This is the simplest and most common form of business. A large proportion of shops and service trades (such as plumbers, electricians and shoe repairers) or establishments (such as cafés and launderettes) are under the control of sole proprietors.

The term 'sole proprietor' does not mean that no-one else works in the business except the owner. Many sole proprietors employ assistants. Rather, the term means that a single person is responsible for raising the capital and managing the business. The owner takes all the profits resulting or bears responsibility if the firm suffers a loss.

Capital

When a person starts a business, it is necessary to estimate how much capital will be required to obtain premises, equipment and a stock of goods. Having arrived at a figure, consideration must then be given to ways of raising money.

The sole proprietor's own savings provide the most satisfactory form of capital. The use of savings reduces the sole proprietor's costs because *interest* payments would have to be paid on borrowed money.

Personal savings may be supplemented by *loans* of money from friends or relatives, from a bank, or from a building society or a finance house if the proprietor intends to buy premises. Finally, it may be possible to obtain *credit* from suppliers. The purchase of stock on credit is similar to obtaining a loan from the supplier for the length of the period of credit.

Once the business is established it may be developed by ploughing back much of the profit made each year.

Advantages of sole proprietorships

- A person who is independent is likely to make more effort than someone working for others in return for a wage or salary. Self-interest is a powerful driving force and the reward for effort belongs wholly to the owner.
- A small business can be effectively managed by the owner. There are no partners or directors to consult, so decisions can be speedily made and put into effect.
- The sole proprietor is in personal contact with customers. Consequently, both their requirements and their credit-worthiness can be readily assessed. In addition, custom may be gained through the owner's own personality and reputation.
- In a small business a more personal relationship is possible between proprietor and employees. In the larger forms of business organisation a lack of understanding frequently exists between management and workers. The close relationship between employer and employee in a sole trader's business enables each of them to understand better the other's point of view.

Disadvantages of sole proprietorships

- The proprietor is personally liable for any debts incurred by the business. This liability extends to private possessions, so that even a house and furniture might have to be sold.
- Control of the business by one person may hinder the development of the firm. A person might be, for example, a first class carpenter, but lacking in managerial ability, or

knowledge of accounts, and the business may not prosper because of the owner's deficiencies. The success or failure of a sole proprietorship depends on one person, whereas in the case of the larger organisations, the personal element is not so evident.

- Scarcity of capital may limit the growth of the business.

Sole proprietorships are suitable for a person with limited capital. When a sole trader's business increases and prospers, consideration will be given to the formation of a partnership or a private company.

8.2 Partnerships

There are two types of partnership: limited partnership and ordinary partnership.

Limited partnership
Under the Limited Partnership Act of 1907, a limited partner's liability for the debts of the firm is restricted to the amount of capital personally invested in the business. However, in a limited partnership there must be at least one ordinary partner whose liability is unlimited. This type of partnership is quite rare.

Ordinary partnership
Ordinary partnerships are governed by the Partnership Act of 1890 and to some extent by the Companies Acts.

Organisation

A partnership is a group of people who carry on business with the purpose of making a profit. Generally the number of partners may vary from a minimum of two to a maximum of twenty. However, under the Companies Acts, unlimited membership is available to *ordinary* partnerships of solicitors, accountants and stockbrokers. Unlimited membership is available to *limited* partnerships of surveyors, auctioneers, valuers and estate agents.

People wishing to form themselves into a partnership should draw up a Partnership Deed of Agreement, which sets out in written form the terms and conditions of the partnership. The Deed should include such items as:

- the names of the partners;
- the amount of capital contributed by each;
- the arrangements for sharing of profits or losses.

The Deed is not a legal necessity when a partnership is formed, but it has the advantage of containing a written agreement should a dispute over the terms of the partnership arise. If there is no Deed of Agreement, then the rights and duties of the partners are determined by the Partnership Act (1890). For example, if there is no written agreement as to sharing profits or losses, the Act lays down that they shall be shared equally.

All the partners have equal powers and responsibilities. For example:

- each partner may bind the firm in any contract made on behalf of the partnership;
- each partner is entitled to take an active part in the management of the firm;
- all the partners are together liable for the debts of the firm to the full extent of their private possessions.

Advantages of partnerships

- The formation of a partnership increases the capital available to an existing sole proprietorship so that the business may be expanded.
- The management of the business can be improved by introducing partners with specialist skills. For example, a qualified accountant could be admitted as a partner to take charge of the financial side of the business.
- The admission of new partners can introduce new ideas and thinking into the business, so that the efficiency of the firm is increased.
- Business decisions can be taken rapidly because partners are working in the business together, and personal contact is possible with both customers and employees.
- Partnerships, like sole traders, are exempted from filing their accounts with the Registrar of Companies. Business owners may dislike making their accounts available for scrutiny, on the grounds that turnover and profit figures give clues to competitors about the profitability of particular products or services, and a firm's share of the market.

Disadvantages of partnerships

Compared with the larger forms of business organisation, partnerships suffer from a number of drawbacks.

- Like sole traders, ordinary partnerships are subject to unlimited liability so that partners are together personally liable for the whole of the debts of the firm. Under a limited partnership, only one partner need take this risk, but in return for having their liability limited to capital invested, limited partners lose the right to take part in the management of the business.
- Any partner may bind the firm in trading contracts and, in this way, commit the other partners. Thus a partner with faulty business judgement or low integrity could damage the business by unwise actions.
- Like sole proprietorship, this type of business lacks continuity of existence. A partnership is automatically dissolved on the death or bankruptcy of a partner. Similarly, by giving notice to the others, a partner can dissolve the partnership at any time.
- Except for firms of accountants, solicitors and stockbrokers (see page 87), the number of partners is limited to 20. The amount of capital subscribed even by 20 partners may not allow the business to expand to its fullest extent.
- Finally, the consent of all the partners is required for the admission of a new partner, and individual obstinacy could very well hinder the development of the business by hindering the admission of very desirable 'new blood'.

Scope of partnerships

Partnerships exist in undertakings where professional skill is of greater importance than amount of capital. In manufacturing, which requires expensive equipment, the partnership is not a suitable type of organisation. However, many professional people such as doctors, dentists and solicitors work in partnerships. People who sell services require relatively little capital compared with those who undertake the production of goods. Some professional people work in partnerships because rules made by their governing bodies do not allow members to form limited companies.

8.3　Limited Companies

The limited company can be described as a group of persons who have joined together in order to carry out some kind of business enterprise, the actual management of the firm being in the hands of a director or board of directors. The capital of the company is divided into shares, normally £1 shares, and profits are divided among the shareholders in proportion to the number of shares held. Sometimes a limited company is called a *joint-stock company*, indicating that a number of people have contributed to a common stock of capital to be used for a business purpose. The word 'limited' means that each member's liability is limited to the amount of capital subscribed. There are two kinds of limited companies: namely, *private* and *public*.

Private companies

Organisation
1　At one time, a private company was allowed to have a minimum of two members and a maximum of fifty but since the Companies Act (1980) there has been no upper limit on membership.
2　Each shareholder has *limited liability*; that is, if the company fails the shareholders are responsible for the debts only up to the amount they hold in shares.
3　This type of company cannot invite the public to subscribe capital.
4　Previously shares could not be transferred without the consent of the directors. However, since the Companies Act (1980), this restriction is no longer compulsory, although share transfer may be restricted, if desired, by a rule written into the articles of association. As a result, shares in private companies cannot be bought or sold on a stock exchange.
5　Despite the description 'private', a complete set of company accounts has to be sent each year to the Registrar of Companies.

Uses
The restriction on sales of shares to the public makes this type of company unsuitable for an undertaking requiring large amounts of capital. The owners of small or medium-sized 'family' businesses often form themselves into a private company. As the minimum number of members is two, a husband and wife can be

the two shareholders. Only one director need be appointed. Clearly, a private company with limited liability for each shareholder has distinct advantages over a partnership.

Public companies

Organisation
1 A minimum of two persons is required to form a public company and there is no upper limit to the number of members. The number of shareholders may be very large indeed and as it would be impossible for them all to manage the business, a committee or *board of directors* is elected to carry out this task. The control of the company is, therefore, delegated to directors (a minimum of two directors must be appointed). A meeting of shareholders must be called at least once a year and at the meeting the accounts of the company must be submitted to the shareholders for their approval. Shareholders can criticise the directors and vote on proposals put forward for discussion.
2 Each shareholder has limited liability.
3 Shares are freely transferable and can be bought and sold on a stock exchange.
4 An appeal can be made to the public to subscribe capital.
5 A copy of the accounts must be sent every year to the Registrar of Companies.
6 The abbreviation *PLC* (public limited company) must appear after the name of the company, e.g. Marks and Spencer PLC, wherever it is displayed. This requirement does not apply to private companies.

Formation of a limited company

People who wish to form a company must carry out certain legal requirements.

In the first place, the name, objects, amount of the authorised capital, and certain other information must be stated in the *memorandum of association*. This is a document which is sent to the Registrar of Companies. There must be at least two subscribers for either a private company or a public company. The memorandum forms the legal framework or *constitution* of the company.

In addition to the memorandum, the Registrar requires a statement of the rules for running the company. These are laid down in the *articles of association*, which deal with such matters as procedure in calling meetings of shareholders, arrangements for the division of profits and so on.

When the memorandum and articles have been inspected and approved, the Registrar will issue a *certificate of incorporation* which gives the company a legal existence. A private company can now commence business, but a public company still has to obtain its capital from the public before it can start business.

The document inviting the public to subscribe capital in the form of shares is known as the *prospectus*. It gives essential facts on which investors may judge the prospects of the company. In order to safeguard investors against false or extravagant claims about the company, a copy of the prospectus has to be sent to the Registrar.

The prospectus must state the minimum amount of capital that is necessary to enable the company to start business. When the Registrar is satisfied that the company's share of capital meets the legal requirements, a *trading certificate* will be issued so that the company may commence business.

The capital of a public company

Capital may be classified as either share capital or loan capital.

Share capital
When a company is formed, it can issue shares up to the amount written into the memorandum of association. This figure is knows as its *authorised capital*. The directors may, however, decide to issue only part of the authorised capital so that a reserve is available for issue at some future date. The part of the authorised capital for which the company invites public subscription is known as the *issued capital*. There must be a minimum issued capital of £50,000.

The share capital of a public company is usually divided into *preference* and *ordinary shares*.

Preference shares This type of share has first claim on any profits and carries a fixed rate of dividend. If the company goes into liquidation, preference shareholders receive repayment of their capital before other shareholders. But, as preference shareholders run less risk, they have less favourable voting rights than other shareholders.

Most issues of preference shares are *cumulative*, which means that if there are insufficient profits in any year to pay the preference dividend, the amount owing to the preference shareholders is carried forward or 'accumulated' until the company is able to pay.

There are also *participating preference shares*, which receive not only a fixed dividend, but in addition, if profits are sufficient, an additional dividend after payment has been made to subordinate classes of shares.

Most shares cannot be bought back by the company so that a shareholder who wishes to dispose of a holding must sell through a broker on the stock exchange. *Redeemable preference shares* are the only type of shares that can be re-purchased by the company. However, they are repaid when the company decides to do so, and not when shareholders want them to be.

The various types of preference shares may be combined, for example: cumulative participating redeemable preference shares.

Ordinary shares　These shares are often referred to as 'equities'. Usually they do not carry a fixed rate of dividend and their holders are paid a dividend only after the claims of preference shareholders have been met. Ordinary shares are also last in the line for return of the money invested if the company goes into liquidation. If profits are good then the ordinary share dividend will be high. On the other hand, in bad years the dividend may be low or even non-existent. Holders of ordinary shares, therefore, bear most of the risk and in consequence have superior voting rights in the company.

A third type of share is more risky still. *Deferred shares* (or founders' or managers' shares) do not receive any dividend until all other types of shares have been paid a certain amount first. Deferred shares are taken up by the promoters of a company because of the valuable voting rights attaching to them. This class of share is comparatively rare.

The issue of shares
There are four ways in which a company can issue shares.

1 The first is termed an *offer for sale*. The issue of shares is purchased by a merchant bank or a stockbroker and then all or part is offered to the public at a slightly higher price.
2 The second method is by means of a *placing*. Thus a stockbroker may buy a block of shares from a company in order to

resell to clients. This method is normally used only in the case of smaller companies.

3 A company which is already in existence may offer additional shares to its shareholders at a price lower than the current market price. The offer is termed a *rights issue*.

4 The method most frequently used is a *public issue*, which is often done through a merchant bank. Investors are invited through the prospectus to apply for stated amounts of the shares at fixed prices.

Very often arrangements are made for the issue to be *underwritten*. This means that the promoters agree with certain large investors, such as banks and insurance companies, that the latter should be responsible for a certain amount of the issue if the whole issue is not subscribed. For example, if only 25% of an issue is taken up by the public, the remainder is taken up and paid for by the underwriters. For their service of guaranteeing to take up capital which is not subscribed by the public, the underwriters receive a commission.

There are a number of stages in a public issue of shares.

- *On application*, investors are required to send a sum of money (e.g. 25p) for every £1 share applied for. If the issue is over-subscribed some intending investors may get no shares or may receive only part of the total number of shares applied for.
- *Allotment* takes place when applicants are informed that they can obtain a certain number of shares. A further payment is due on allotment (e.g. 25p).
- The balance owing (e.g. 50p) is payable by a number of *calls*. Thus a first call for another 25p may be made and later, a second and final call for 25p. Sometimes uncalled capital is used to provide a reserve of additional capital. The shareholders are liable for the amount of uncalled capital and the balance is payable when the directors 'call' for it. The actual amount of capital that shareholders have subscribed is called *paid-up* capital.

Payment for shares may, therefore, be spread over a period of months. Once the full value has been paid, no further claims can be made on shareholders because their liability is limited to the capital invested.

Each shareholder is issued with a *share certificate* showing the number and class of shares held.

Loan capital

In addition to share capital, a company may raise funds by long-term borrowing.

Debentures may be issued on the security of the company's property. Debentures are not shares and the holders are not members of the company and do not have voting rights. They are creditors and must be paid their fixed rate of interest whether the company makes a profit or not and before any dividend is paid on shares. If the company fails to pay interest or repay the loan, debenture holders may sell the business in order to recover their money.

Loans without security are often referred to as *loan stock*.

Thus debentures and loan stock bring capital into the company without extending the basis of ownership.

Finance corporations are an important source of long-term loan capital. Examples are as follows.

- *The Finance Corporation for Industry* (FCI) which provides loans for larger companies.
- The *Industrial and Commercial Finance Corporation* (ICFC) which assists smaller firms by providing loans (or ordinary share capital). Both FCI and ICFC are backed by the same holding company known as *Investors in Industry*.
- The Ventures Division of *Investors in Industry* provides finance for the commercial development of worthwhile technical innovations involving greater risks than existing organisations are prepared to take.

(The three institutions outlined above are jointly owned by, or have the backing of, the Bank of England and the commercial banks or insurance companies.)

Another method of raising money is to *mortgage* the property owned by the company. A mortgage deed is drawn up and the money borrowed on the security of the property is repaid with interest over a period of years.

Government aid in the form of loans or grants is available to firms which will expand in areas of high unemployment.

All of the forms of loan capital outlined above provide long-term finance, often over twenty years or more. Temporary increases of capital may be provided by the following means:

- an extension of *credit* facilities from suppliers (the purchase of stock on credit for a number of months is the same thing as obtaining a loan for the length of the period of credit);

- a bank *overdraft* is a form of loan granted for periods up to twelve months, after which time borrowing facilities may be renewed (see Chapter 13);
- the sale of trade debts to a specialist firm known as a factor. *Factoring* enables the seller to exchange the right to a future payment for present cash. A variation of this practice known as *invoice discounting* is borrowing against the security of book debts.

Finally, a company may increase its capital by *ploughing back* a proportion of the profit made each year; by *leasing*; and by *hire purchase*.

Both leasing and hire purchase enable firms to obtain the use of equipment without having to spend large amounts on purchasing it. Whereas under hire purchase the user of the equipment eventually becomes the owner (see page 66), under leasing this is not generally the case. A lease is a contract giving the use of equipment for a certain period of time. The lessee pays rent to the owner (or lessor) and ownership remains with the latter. Finance for leasing and hire purchase is supplied by finance houses and banks. Most forms of equipment – vehicles, office furniture, computers, machinery – can be leased. Although the lessee does not obtain ownership of the equipment, the system permits up-dating when an item becomes obsolete.

Advantages of public companies

- Larger amounts of capital can be raised than is possible with other forms of business organisation. Capital running into many millions of pounds may be raised from a great many people, allowing production on a large scale.
- The capital may be divided into different kinds of shares each of which carries a different degree of risk. Hence an appeal is made to different groups of investors.
- All the shareholders enjoy limited liability. This privilege encourages people with only small sums available for investment to subscribe to the joint 'stock' of capital.
- Legal regulations safeguard the interest of shareholders and persons dealing with the company. For example, when a company is formed, the memorandum and articles of association must be inspected by the Registrar of Companies before a Certificate of Incorporation is issued. Again, at the end of each year of trading, a copy of the accounts must be

submitted to the Registrar, and this publicity is a safeguard against fraud.

- Shareholders may dispose of their shares easily and quickly through the London and provincial stock exchanges. This fact encourages people to invest and makes it easier for companies to obtain new capital.
- Unlike sole proprietorships and partnerships, the public company has a continuous existence. It exists as a legal entity quite apart from the individuals who hold the shares, and is unaffected by the death of even the largest shareholder. One company can own the shares of another company and a company formed in one country, e.g. Britain, may own shares in another country, e.g. the United States. Similarly a foreign-owned company can own shares in a British company. The term *multinational* is used to describe a company which owns assets in more than one country.

Disadvantages of public companies

Despite their many advantages, public companies suffer from a number of drawbacks.

- The personal element which may be characteristic of smaller business units is lacking. Employees often feel that they are mere 'units of labour' and that the company's profit is more important than their welfare. In fairness, it must be pointed out that many companies have acknowledged this criticism. Personnel departments have been set up in an effort to bridge the gap between management and employees. Welfare schemes and social amenities also represent the efforts of companies in this direction.
- The major concern of most shareholders is the amount of their dividend. Consequently they may show little interest in other important factors such as employees' working conditions, export performance and modernisation of equipment.
- Ownership and control become separated. Whereas the firm's assets are owned by the shareholders, it is the directors who control the policy of the firm. Directors may be removed by the shareholders and new directors elected, but this can be done only at the *annual general meeting* or at an *extraordinary meeting*.
- The large size of companies leads to problems of management and control. The larger the firm, the more necessary are rules

and regulations. Hence (*a*) individual initiative may be discouraged or restricted in scope and (*b*) quick decisions may not be possible and delays may occur.

8.4　Franchising

People who start a business – whether in the form of a sole tradership, partnership or limited company – have to work hard and long to become established and well-known. Some people choose to buy themselves into a well-known organisation such as Budget Car Rental, Wimpy Bars, Dyno-Rod, Midas Exhaust or Prontaprint by means of a franchise agreement.

A franchise is a licence to sell a product or service. Over 100 companies in Great Britain offer franchises. They issue a licence – together with their trade name, business expertise, advertising and other services – to provide a tried and tested product, in a particular place for a specified time.

In order to obtain a franchise an initial lump sum of money is usually payable. There may also be royalty payments to the company which provided the franchise, and raw materials usually have to be bought from the company.

Although franchising can eliminate the risks faced when setting up a new business alone, inevitably some independence is forfeited. Whilst the franchise holder owns the business, the franchisor (*a*) will not allow any alteration in the way in which the franchise arrangement operates; (*b*) retains the right of intervention to maintain standards and encourage progress.

8.5　Co-operatives

The characteristic features of a co-operative retail society were considered in Section 2.5. Whereas companies are subject to the Companies Acts, co-operative societies are organised under the Industrial and Provident Societies Acts as *Friendly Societies*. They have the status of corporate bodies with full legal powers. Like companies, they are required to make returns to a Registrar.

Figure 8.1 demonstrates how public companies and co-operative societies differ.

Fig. 8.1 *Co-operative societies and public companies*

	Co-operative Retail Society	Public Company
Ownership	The owners are the customers.	The owners are not necessarily the customers.
	Regional/localised ownership.	Possibly national/ international ownership.
	Shareholders may contribute capital up to a fixed amount.	There is no limit on a member's shareholding and one or a few shareholders may hold the majority of shares.
	Shareholders receive a twofold income: (*a*) nterest on share capital (*b*) dividend on purchases.	Shareholders receive a share in the profits according to the size of their shareholding.
Control	Each shareholder has one vote irrespective of the capital held.	Usually the shareholders have votes in proportion to their capital holdings.
	A society is managed by a committee elected by the shareholders.	Control is by a board of directors elected by the shareholders.
Raising Capital	Normally one type of share with fixed interest.	Different types of shares receive different proportions of profits.
	Share capital can be withdrawn from the society at short notice.	A company does not normally repay capital and a holder must dispose of shares by selling them to someone else.
	Remains constant in value.	Quoted on stock exchange and may vary in value.
Disposal of Profits	Profits shared among owner/customers.	Profits distributed among owners who may buy little or nothing from the business.
	Many employees are members.	May have profit sharing schemes for employees.
Law	Subject to the Industrial and Provident Societies Acts.	Subject to the Companies Acts.

Workers' co-operatives

This form of business is owned and democratically controlled by the members, who are mainly or entirely employees. Co-operative businesses differ from other kinds of business because they use certain operating principles.

- Membership is open to all employees.
- Members have equal voting rights irrespective of their financial involvement.
- The return on any investment is limited to a reasonable rate.
- Any profits are distributed according to the work put in, not according to money invested.

Most co-operatives register as a corporate body with limited liability, either through incorporation under the Companies Acts or by registration under the Industrial and Provident Societies Acts.

Among the benefits claimed for co-operatives are enhanced job satisfaction; minimal conflict, because workers and owners are one and the same; high quality products or services, due to increased motivation; and a greater awareness of business realities among members. However, members of co-operatives require a considerable amount of dedication and commitment. Members must be prepared to take responsibility and participate in the running of the business.

Scope of co-operatives
Co-operatives are engaged in a wide range of activities, such as servicing computer software, clothing manufacture, building services, electronic engineering and advertising.

Test Yourself

1 Name the simplest and most common form of business organisation in Britain.
2 List the possible sources of a sole proprietor's capital.
3 Write down the advantages enjoyed by a sole trader.
4 There are two types of partnership. What are they?
5 How do the Companies Acts affect the maximum number allowed in a partnership?
6 What is a Partnership Deed of Agreement?
7 Name the major drawback of both sole proprietorships and partnerships.

8 Briefly describe the characteristics of a business organised as a partnership.
9 What is the meaning of 'joint stock' companies?
10 Why is a company described as 'limited'?
11 In what sense can a private company be said to be 'private'?
12 Name the types of undertaking for which a private company is (*a*) unsuitable, (*b*) very suitable.
13 Write down the minimum number of members necessary to form a public company.
14 Name the two documents which must be sent to the Registrar by the promoters of a company.
15 Which two documents must be issued by the Registrar to a public company before it can begin trading?
16 Name the document advertising a public issue of shares.
17 Name three kinds of preference shares.
18 Give two reasons why investors may prefer to hold ordinary shares rather than preference shares.
19 Define a debenture.
20 Give the three stages in buying shares from a company.
21 Name three finance corporations.
22 Give three ways of providing temporary increases in capital.
23 How do leasing and hire purchase differ?
24 What is a multinational company?
25 List two ways in which a co-operative society differs from a public company.
26 How do workers' co-operatives differ from other kinds of business?

Chapter 9

Public Ownership

A large share of all goods and services is produced by public undertakings operated by the state or by local authorities.

9.1 Public Corporations

Undertakings controlled by the state are organised as public corporations. Some corporations (such as the British Broadcasting Corporation and the Port of London Authority) were established before the Second World War (1939-45). Between 1945 and 1951 several industries were *nationalised* and these also were organised as public corporations. Nationalisation means the taking over, by the state, of established undertakings which are being run as private concerns. Post-war nationalisation included major sections of the *fuel* and *power*, *transport* and *steel* industries.

The *Bank of England* and the *Post Office* are also state undertakings. The Bank was nationalised in 1946; but as the central bank, it had worked closely with the government for very many years. The Post Office, throughout its long history, has been a public institution. Until 1969 it was operated as a government department, but it is now a public corporation.

When an industry is *privatised* (or denationalised) it is returned to private ownership. Since 1980 a number of nationalised industries have been privatised. The controlling bodies (public corporations) have been converted into public companies and shares sold to investors. Examples of privatisation include the National Freight Corporation, British Telecom and British Airways.

Organisation and control

Although there are certain differences of detail in the organisation of nationalised industries, the bodies which control them are all *public corporations*. The sphere of each corporation's operations is contained in an Act of Parliament, which also places the corporation under the control of a minister responsible to Parliament.

The chairman and members of a public corporation are appointed (and may be dismissed) by the minister of the appropriate government department. For example, the members of the Board of British Rail are appointed by the Minister of Transport. The corporation is the central authority for the industry and is answerable to the minister, and through the minister to parliament, for its efficiency.

Although ministers do not interfere in the day-to-day working of nationalised industries, these large-scale organisations are subject to a substantial measure of government control. Each corporation is required to prepare an annual report and submit it to the minister, who may be questioned on it in Parliament.

Capital and profits

When the government took over the industries mentioned above, the former shareholders were compensated for the loss of their shares by the issue of an appropriate amount of nationalised industry stock. The stock carries the government's guarantee and earns a fixed rate of interest. This means that holders of the stock receive interest whether the industry makes a profit or a loss. Shareholders in a public company receive dividends only when the company makes a profit, but normally the dividend is not fixed so that when profits are good, they may receive a high return on their investment.

A nationalised industry has the power to raise capital by issuing stock and by borrowing money from the commercial banks. These borrowings are covered by government guarantee. In practice, much of the corporations' capital comes from their own commercial profits and from government loans.

If a nationalised industry makes a *profit*, it cannot distribute a dividend because there are no shareholders. Instead it can do one or more of several things:

- decrease the prices charged to consumers and so eliminate the surplus of income over expenditure;
- raise the wages paid to employees in the industry which will increase costs and so help eliminate any profit;
- use the surplus to finance capital development.

Losses made by public corporations have to be financed by government grants.

In order to represent consumers' interests, councils have been established for most of the nationalised industries. Each consumer council comprises members appointed by the minister. Nominations to the minister are put forward by local authorities, trade associations and other bodies judged to be representative of consumers.

The work of a council is twofold: to deal with complaints and suggestions from consumers; and to advise the minister of consumers' views.

Fig. 9.1   *Differences between a public company and a public corporation*

Company		Corporation
Owned by shareholders who elect directors to manage the company.	Ownership	Owned by state; members of controlling authority appointed by minister of appropriate government department.
Ultimate control resides in voting power of shareholders. Accounts must be presented annually to shareholders.	Control	Annual report submitted to the responsible minister who may be questioned on it in Parliament.
Appeal to investors. Success depends on how the latter judge its shares.	Raising of Capital	Power to raise capital and borrow money with government guarantee.
Profits distributed among shareholders in proportion to type and number of shares held.	Disposal of Profits	No shareholders. Profit retained as capital, or disposed of by reducing prices or paying higher wages.

9.2   Municipal Undertakings

Local authorities provide and administer a number of essential services such as education, health and welfare, housing, fire services and recreation facilities. In addition, local authorities are also involved in trading enterprises. For example, Hull operates its own telephone service and in Birmingham there is a Municipal Bank. Other local authority enterprises include the operation of baths and swimming pools, abattoirs and markets, restaurants and sports facilities and, particularly in seaside towns, the provision of entertainment and other facilities for visitors.

Organisation and control

Control of municipal trading undertakings is exercised through a trading *committee* composed of councillors who delegate authority for the day-to-day running to salaried municipal officials. The latter are answerable to the *committee* for all matters affecting the undertaking.

Capital and profits

The initial capital for a municipal undertaking is often provided by *borrowing*. The local authority has to apply to the Department of the Environment to raise a loan for a particular purpose. If the project is approved, the money will be raised by: an issue of *stock*; application to the *Public Works Loan Board*; issuing *mortgages*; or by issuing *bonds*, usually for one year.

Profits made by municipal undertakings may be used to relieve the *rates*. (This source of income of a local authority comes from rates levied at so many pence in the pound on the rateable value of property within its area.) However, if the enterprise runs at a *loss*, this is borne by the ratepayers.

9.3 Advantages of Public Undertakings

The arguments in favour of the production of goods and services by state and municipal enterprises are as follows.

- Nationalisation enables the working of an industry to be planned as a whole. Before transport was nationalised, the competing railway companies often constructed two or even three railway lines between the two places. In the 18th and 19th centuries, canals were built with varying widths, bridge heights and lock sizes. Consequently only a very small canal boat can travel right across the country. This haphazard development of means of transport resulted in a great waste of resources. Thus, it is argued, nationalised industries which are the sole suppliers of the various services can avoid wasteful duplication of railway lines, electricity cables and so on.

- Privately owned undertakings operate in order to earn a profit for their shareholders. However, a nationalised industry without shareholders can take account of other objectives. For example, trains may be run on certain lines for the convenience of people living in the area, although the service may run at loss. Coal mines which work at a loss may be kept open in order to provide employment in certain areas. Similarly, a local authority may subsidise swimming facilities on the grounds that a high charge for admission may deprive poorer members of the community of the use of this facility.
- Certain industries such as coal and transport are *basic industries*, that is, many other industries depend on them. It may be argued that if the basic industries were privately owned, the owners might exploit their key position by regulating the supply and prices of their products in order to earn excess profits.
- Successful municipal trading enterprises may lead to a reduction in the rates. Low rates in a district may attract new industries to it and so increase its prosperity.

9.4   Criticisms of Public Undertakings

The opponents of state control claim the system has many disadvantages.

- The immense size of nationalised industries creates problems of management and control. In turn, efforts to control these giant enterprises lead to 'red-tape', form-filling and impersonal labour relationships.
- People work hardest when they work for themselves – that is, when their own capital is at risk. In a nationalised industry, the people in control are salaried employees and they may show less managerial drive than exists in a private business.
- Privately owned businesses compete with each other to sell goods and services. Consequently they endeavour to keep costs and prices as low as possible in order to do better than rival firms. A nationalised industry usually has a legal *monopoly*, that is, similar undertakings cannot be set up in competition. Lack of competition may lead to inefficiency and higher prices than would be the case under private enterprise.
- Nationalised industries may be heavily subsidised so that they become a drain upon the taxpayers. The latter have not the same opportunities for criticism as have shareholders in a limited company.

Test Yourself

1 Name two nationalised industries in Britain.
2 Name the type of organisation which runs a nationalised industry.
3 Who is responsible for the management of a nationalised industry?
4 Who bears the risks of state undertakings?
5 How were the former shareholders compensated when an industry was nationalised?
6 What advantage does a state undertaking possess over private enterprise in the raising of capital?
7 What are the ways in which a state undertaking can make use of any profit?
8 Name as many examples as you can of trading enterprises run by local authorities.
9 How are municipal undertakings controlled?
10 Name an important source of income of a local authority.
11 How can nationalisation prevent wastage of resources?
12 Why would a privately owned enterprise be unable to provide a service on social grounds?
13 List four possible drawbacks of state enterprise.

Chapter 10

Stock Exchanges

A market where stocks, shares and other kinds of securities are bought and sold is called a *stock exchange*. Stock exchanges are to be found in financial centres throughout the world – London, New York (Wall Street), Paris (the Bourse), etc. They maintain close contact with each other by means of the telephone, telex and other data transmission services.

In Britain, the origins of the Stock Exchange (now termed the International Stock Exchange) can be traced back to the 18th century when the government and trading enterprises began to seek to raise money by public subscription. Stocks and shares were issued and, as they were bought and sold on an increasing scale, a regular market began to form in London. Today the London Stock Exchange is the most important market in shares in Britain although the major provincial financial centres (such as Birmingham, Newcastle and Manchester) also have exchanges.

10.1 Organisation

Business inside the London Stock Exchange is conducted only by members of the Exchange who are broker/dealers. The Exchange is governed by a Council whose members are elected by members of the Stock Exchange.

Member firms act as agents for investors who wish to buy or sell shares. The same firm can also buy and sell shares for itself and try to make a profit. This ability to carry out two types of trading is known as 'dual capacity'.

Some broker/dealers also specialise as market makers. These firms are prepared to buy or sell shares at all times.

Types of securities

In addition to shares, debentures (see page 95) and stocks are dealt in on the Exchange. *Stocks* are securities sold to raise loans for the government, local authorities or overseas governments. Stocks are usually quoted per £100 nominal value, but fractions may be bought or sold, whereas shares are not divisible. Stocks are also known as *bonds*.

Broker/dealers and market makers

When broker/dealer firms act as agents for investors, they receive instructions from their clients to buy or sell shares; and then have to ensure that the documents are properly processed and the money accounted for and paid over. In addition, broker/dealers provide their clients with advice and guidance about their investments. For these services broker/dealers are paid by means of a *commission* charged on business transacted.

Market makers do not deal directly with investors. They are principals to whom the broker/dealers come to buy or sell their clients' shares. Since there are so many different issues, market makers tend to specialise in particular kinds such as banks, steel firms, oil companies and so on. Market makers obtain their income from the *profit* (known as the *turn*) they make in buying and re-selling shares.

The market maker's function of acting as a wholesaler and holding a stock of shares permits shares to be bought and sold at any time. A holder of shares can easily turn them into cash, and this is an important consideration for investors when they are considering the purchase of a new issue of shares.

The holding of stocks by market makers means also that prices tend to be steadier. The market maker specialises in certain types of share, and acquires a specialist knowledge. If, therefore, demand causes share prices to rise, the market maker will at some stage sell in order to make a profit, thus releasing more shares on to the market. Thus supply is increased as demand is increasing. Similarly, when investors sell shares and prices are falling, market makers will tend to buy, thus taking quantities of shares out of the market. Demand increases, therefore, as supply increases and the effect in both cases is to even out price fluctuations, making the market more stable.

Investors

An investor who has subscribed to an issue of debentures has *lent* money to the company. An investor who buys shares in a company becomes *owner* of a part of the company and its assets. In either case, the company records the investor's name and address in a register. These records are used to send out dividend or interest payments, as well as copies of the annual report and accounts, and letters and circulars.

An investor in a public company, who wishes to sell shares or debentures, must find a buyer, and the simplest way of doing this is to employ a broker/dealer.

There are certain advantages for an investor who sells or buys shares through a broker/dealer. In the first place, a broker is a specialist who can advise on the merits of particular shares and on when to buy and sell to the best advantage. In addition, a broker/dealer possesses expert knowledge on how to transfer ownership from one person to another.

Secondly, a broker/dealer can buy or sell shares more cheaply than could the buyer or owner acting for themselves. By dealing for a large number of clients and by spreading costs a broker/dealer can work for a relatively small commission.

Dealing in shares

A broker/dealer who received an order from a client to buy shares in a particular company contacts the market makers who specialise in the shares of that company. The use of information technology permits a market maker to display current buying and selling prices on terminals accessible anywhere in Britain – and indeed the world. This screen dealing system means that a broker/dealer can tell at the touch of a button what are the latest prices offered by competing market makers in any particular security. Those market makers who are more keen to sell than buy shares will quote a lower price than those who prefer to buy and a deal will be made with the one who quotes the lowest price. If the broker/dealer had been instructed to sell, the deal would have been made with the market maker offering the highest price.

In order to protect investors, all information on trading and prices is stored by electronic dealing systems. The availability for later inspection of this information should ensure that deals are done to the best advantage of the investors. The bargain is notified to the broker/dealer's client by means of a *contract note* which gives details of the shares bought and the broker/dealer's commission. A date on the contract note tells the client when payment for the shares is required and with most share transactions this will be on a settlement day a short time ahead.

The selling broker/dealer sends a completed *stock transfer form* to the company whose shares are involved so that dividends and communications may be sent in due course. The form identifies the previous owner of the shares and the new owners.

The seller's *share certificate* is sent back to the company for cancellation and is replaced by a new one made out in the name of the buyer. The share certificate signifies that the person whose name appears on it is a part owner of the company and that this fact has been entered in the company's register.

In addition to providing evidence that a broker/dealer has carried out the client's instructions, a contract note serves another purpose: it fixes the date of the transaction. This is particularly important when a company is about to pay a dividend or distribute new shares to its shareholders as a *rights issue*. Some weeks before the payment of- a dividend the company, in order to provide time to prepare the dividend warrants, has to fix a date to determine the list of shareholders who will receive payment. The Stock Exchange has then to fix another date, known as the *ex-dividend* (*ex-div.*) date to allow time for documents arising from recent transactions to reach the company for inclusion in the payment list. Any person who buys shares before the ex-dividend date is said to have bought *cum-dividend* (*cum-div.*) and is entitled to receive the value of the dividend (or new share rights).

As noted above, a date on a contract note tells the client when payment for a purchase is required. In the case of government stocks this is usually the next day. For company securities, however, it may be between two and four weeks later. This is because of the system used for dealing and settlement. Dealings for two (or sometimes three) successive weeks are put together in what is known as an *Account* and settled all together on the seventh working day after the end of the Account.

Settlement of deals is completed by a computer network called *Talisman*. Despite the use of a computerised settlement system, share certificates still have to be exchanged. A new settlement system (called *Taurus*) designed to allow stockbrokers and others to transfer shares by computer, replacing existing paperwork, is planned for 1990.

Share prices

The face value of a share is called its *nominal* or *par value*. It may be 25p, £1, £5, or any other amount, and it appears on the share certificate. The *market value* is the price obtained when a share is sold. Thus the market value may be above par or below par or it may be at par when it equals the nominal value.

The market prices of stocks and shares change frequently. The *Daily Official List* published by the Stock Exchange and the abridged lists printed in daily newspapers show the prices at which bargains were made on the Exchange. Selected share prices are also carried on screen services such as *Prestel, Oracle* and *Ceefax* (see Chapter 15).

The market price indicates the level of demand for the shares. The supply of a particular share is virtually fixed by the company's memorandum of association which lays down the amount of the authorised capital. The factors affecting demand for a particular share include investors' expectations of the level of future dividends, rumours of mergers or takeover bids, political conditions and the general economic position of the country.

Unlisted Securities Market (USM)

This special market for shares in small companies was set up by the Stock Exchange. Less stringent rules are applicable than those for companies seeking a quotation or full listing (see Section 10.3). The purpose is to allow small companies access to shareholders' capital. Investors buy and sell shares of USM companies in the same way as they deal in those of fully-listed companies, i.e. through a broker.

In addition to less stringent requirements, the amount of capital which is issued is smaller (10% minimum rather than 25% for a full listing). Consequently the speculative element in the shares is greater. It is the small investor who is particularly active in this market, as the average size of the transaction is far more suited to this level of investment than to institutional investors.

10.2 Speculation

Many people or institutions invest their savings in stocks and shares because they are seeking an *income* in the form of either dividend or interest. Others buy shares partly for this reason but also in the hope that the price of the shares will rise in the future. If this happens the investor can make a *capital gain* or profit. In general, speculators are more concerned with making quick profits from buying and selling than with income from investment.

Speculators deal within the Account, that is within a two or three week period, and usually they have no intention of making or accepting delivery of the shares. Those who buy in anticipation that prices will rise before the next settlement are known as *bulls*. If the shares do in fact rise in price, as the buyer anticipated, they are sold at a profit. On the next settlement day, both transactions are settled by payment of the difference between the purchase price and the selling price. This amount is received from the broker/dealer with whom the speculator dealt. For example, suppose a bull speculator instructs a broker/dealer to buy 500 shares at £1 each. Within a few days, the price rises to £1.20 and the bull now sells the shares for £600. At the settlement the broker/dealer owes the speculator £600, less £500 and the *brokerage* plus expenses.

On the other hand, those who sell in anticipation that prices will fall are called *bears*. If the anticipated fall in price takes place the bear speculator buys the shares back. Hence the difference between the selling price and the lower buying price is owed to the speculator by the broker. Thus if a bear sells 500 shares at £1 and before the end of the Account the price falls to £0.80, the broker/dealer will be asked to buy 500 at that price. Thus the bear speculator receives £500, less £400 and brokerage plus expenses.

The market is said to be a 'bull market' or 'bullish' when share prices are tending to rise; conversely, it is described as a 'bear market' or 'bearish' if prices are generally falling.

If a bull speculator's anticipations turn out to be wrong (e.g. prices go down) settlement of transactions due at the end of the Account may be postponed in return for a charge called *contango* which is paid by the buyer to the seller. Similarly bear speculators may wish to postpone delivery of shares that they have sold, because the anticipated fall in price has not occurred. Delivery may be postponed to the next Account by payment of a charge called *backwardation* to the buyer.

Another group of speculators are known as *stags*. They subscribe to *new issues*, in the hope of selling the shares allotted to them at a profit when dealings commence.

When a new issue takes place the number of shares applied for by investors often exceeds the number to be allotted. The high demand often results in the shares being sold at a *premium*, (that is, at a price higher than the issue price) when dealing opens on the Exchange. A stag tries to anticipate the over-subscription of an issue of new shares and applies for a large number. The purpose is to sell at a profit as soon as possible. This kind of speculation is assisted by the system of paying for new shares in stages (see page 94). For example, £1 shares may be issued on such terms as 20p per share on application, and two further instalments of 40p later. A stag applies for many more shares than could be paid for if the full price were demanded on allotment, and remits 20p for each share. The demand for the new issue may cause the shares to rise, for example, to 30p on the Stock Exchange. Hence the stag sells at this price, ceases to be liable for further instalments and makes a profit of 10p per share. In order to discourage stags, a company may require that the full value of the shares applied for is to be remitted with the application. On the other hand, stag speculators help to ensure that a new issue is fully taken up.

Speculators are to be found on most highly organised markets (see page 63). Their dealings have a number of beneficial effects. On the Stock Exchange the presence of speculators makes it possible for others to sell or buy shares at the times most convenient to them. Without speculators, who will usually buy or sell at any time, investors wishing to turn shares into cash might experience difficulty in finding purchasers. Speculators also tend to render price changes more gradual because they buy when others wish to sell and they sell when others wish to buy.

On the other hand, speculation can have a harmful effect. Since speculators make their profits out of price changes, they may be encouraged to manipulate prices to suit their own interests.

10.3   Functions of a Stock Exchange

1 It provides a market for the purchase and sale of existing shares. If there was no Stock Exchange, investors would have to claim their money back from companies. No business could function under such conditions because assets such as premises or machinery might have to be sold quickly in order to raise money to repay shareholders.
2 It assists in raising new capital for industry. The Exchange itself does not issue shares to the public. (It is, as has been shown, a market for secondhand shares.) But by granting a *listing* or permission to deal in new shares, the Exchange makes it much easier for companies to obtain buyers for new shares. Many investors would not buy new shares unless these had been admitted to listing by the Stock Exchange and could, therefore, be turned easily into cash.
3 It channels savings to reach those who need new finance. In addition to direct investors (that is, those who buy and sell

through brokers) there are many *indirect investors*. These are people whose savings are invested on the Stock Exchange by the institutions which hold them. For example, building societies, the National Savings Bank, the Trustee Savings Bank, insurance companies, co-operative societies and trade unions are *institutional investors*. This great flow of savings comprises the supply of loanable funds which are needed by industry to buy land, buildings, machinery and equipment. The Stock Exchange is the main channel through which government and industry tap this supply of loanable funds for the finance they need to replace their equipment, to expand their production, and to develop new products.

4 It provides a basis for the valuation of shares. The Daily Official List is a list of dealings in, and prices of, all quoted securities which is published by the Exchange every business day. It enables valuations to be made; for instance, for assessing *inheritance transfer tax* payable on a deceased person's shareholding, or for assessing *capital gains tax.*

5 It safeguards the interests of investors. Before being admitted to the status of 'listing', companies must submit themselves to extensive scrutiny, and must agree to keep shareholders properly informed about their progress. In addition, business on the Exchange is conducted only by its members, and according to rules drawn up by the Council of the Exchange. An investor who is faced with financial loss, because a member of the Exchange cannot pay for any reason, is recompensed from the Compensation Fund by the Exchange. Electronic storage of information further enhances investor protection.

6 It facilitates borrowing by the government. Investors who buy government stock know that they can, whenever they wish, turn it into cash by selling on the Exchange.

Test Yourself

1 Give a definition of a stock exchange.
2 Briefly outline the origins of the Stock Exchange.
3 State the main classes of stocks dealt in on the Exchange.
4 What are the functions of a broker/dealer?
5 Briefly describe the work of a market maker.
6 What is the importance of the system of registered share-ownership?
7 What advantages are gained by an investor through dealing with a broker/dealer?

8 Briefly describe the procedure for the purchase or sale of shares.
9 What is a contract note?
10 What is the importance of a share certificate?
11 What is the meaning of (*a*) ex div. and (*b*) cum div.?
12 What period of time is covered by an Account?
13 What is the meaning of (*a*) par value and (*b*) market value?
14 Why is the supply of a particular share virtually fixed?
15 Define (*a*) bulls, (*b*) bears, (*c*) stags.
16 Give the meaning of (*a*) contango and (*b*) backwardation.
17 Does speculation have any beneficial effects?
18 How does the Stock Exchange assist in the raising of new capital?
19 How does the Stock Exchange safeguard the interests of investors?

Chapter 11

The Results of Trading

11.1 Capital

Money used in a business is called capital. The methods of raising capital were noted in Chapters 8 and 9. They are determined by the form of the business organisation concerned. For example, a sole trader will probably obtain capital to start a business from personal savings whereas a public company will offer shares for sale to the public.

Capital owned and capital employed

The money invested by the owner to buy equipment, premises and other items necessary to set up the business is *capital owned*. This amount need not, however, represent the total capital used in a business. In order to supplement personal savings a trader may borrow from a bank or building society. The capital provided by the loan does not belong to the owner and cannot be included in the total capital owned. Similarly, when a trader buys goods on credit, capital is being borrowed from suppliers. The greater the total sum borrowed, the greater will be the excess of *capital used* over capital owned.

Fixed capital

The owner of a business uses part of the capital available to buy *fixed assets* such as premises, machinery, fixtures and fittings, which are essential to trading and will be retained in the business over a long period of time.

Some types of business need more fixed assets than others. For example, the retailer needs more attractive premises than a wholesaler and a greater proportion of a retailer's capital is fixed. A manufacturer requiring extensive premises, machinery and equipment has a bigger proportion of fixed capital than either of the two kinds of trader mentioned above.

Circulating capital (or current assets)

The remainder of the capital (which is still in the form of money) will be used to work the business. A stock of goods will be bought and sold to customers who pay cash which can, in turn, be used to buy more stock. This kind of capital *circulates* and is constantly changing. For example, when a trader makes a sale, cash increases and stock falls.

In the case of a retail or wholesale business, circulating capital consists mainly of *cash*, *debts* and *stocks* of goods. Manufacturers would, however, include a supply of *raw materials* in their circulating capital.

Fig. 11.1   *How a wholesaler's capital works*

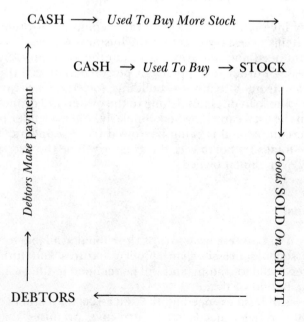

CASH $\longrightarrow$ *Used To Buy More Stock* $\longrightarrow$

CASH $\rightarrow$ *Used To Buy* $\rightarrow$ STOCK

Debtors Make payment

Goods SOLD On CREDIT

DEBTORS $\longleftarrow$

Working capital

This is a term used to describe the resources available to a business for (*a*) buying new equipment and (*b*) paying regular expenses such as wages, the cost of stock, charges for stationery and so on. It is calculated by deducting the total amount owing by the business to its creditors (sometimes called *current liabilities*) from the total of *current assets*. For example, if the current assets of a business comprises cash £250, bank balance £14 750, debtors £10 000 and a stock of goods valued at £12 500; and £5000 is owing to trade creditors, then working capital is as follows:

Current assets (£37 500) minus creditors (£5000) = £32 500.

If the current assets amount to less than the current liabilities then there is no working capital. In this situation, if a trader were called upon to pay amounts owing to creditors all at once this could not be done from current assets. Consequently the trader might be forced to delay settlement and run the risk of acquiring the reputation of being a slow payer. In addition, the trader would lose the benefit of deducting cash discount from payments (see page 34) and shortage of cash might cause the trader to restrict credit to customers.

A shortage of working capital can occur if a firm buys more stock on credit than it can sell in a reasonable time; or if too many orders for sales have been accepted so that extra payments for materials and wages are incurred. In either case, the firm is said to have been *overtrading*.

A lack of working capital can be remedied in two ways. Either purchases must be reduced and sales speeded up so that cash outflow declines and the flow of cash into the business increases; or money must be borrowed. Although the latter remedy increases working capital, it also incurs the additional expense of interest charges.

Balance sheet

At the end of the trading year a trader will draw up a *balance sheet*. This is a statement of the *assets* (items owned) and *liabilities* (items owed) of the business. An example of a balance sheet appears in Figure 11.2. It has been arranged in such a way as to show (*a*) capital owned, (*b*) capital employed, (*c*) working capital.

Fig 11.2   *A balance sheet*

Balance Sheet as at 31 December 19—		£	£	£
Capital Owned				11550
Loan				<u>4500</u>
Capital Employed				£16050
Fixed Assets:	Premises	12000		
	Van	1095		
	Fittings	<u>570</u>		
				13665
Current Assets:	Stock	1260		
	Debtors	552		
	Bank	651		
	Cash	<u>117</u>	2580	
Less Current liabilities: Creditors			<u>195</u>	
Working Capital				<u>2385</u>
Net Value of Assets				£16050

11.2   Turnover

Once a business has been established the principal aim of the owner is to sell goods or services and earn *profit*.

The *turnover* of a business is the total *net sales* (i.e. the sales total less any goods returned by customers) during a period of time, such as a year.

The rate of turnover (or *stockturn*) is the number of times the average stock is sold during a period of time. For example, a newsagent purchases a stock of newspapers every morning and sells them the same day. The stock is sold once a day. Greengrocers and fishmongers will often replenish their stock daily but a furniture retailer has a much slower rate of turnover. This is because furniture lasts a long time and is bought infrequently by consumers.

The rate of turnover can be calculated by dividing the average stock into the value of sales at cost price as follows:

$$\text{Rate of turnover} = \frac{\text{Sales at cost}}{\text{Average stock}}$$

Thus if net sales at cost price are £10 000 and the average stock is valued at £2000, the rate of turnover is 5. This means that £2000 worth of stock can be sold five times in a year. The average time that any article remains in stock before being sold is 2.4 months.

Average stock is calculated by adding the value of stock at the beginning of a financial period to the value of stock held at the end of the same trading period. The total is divided by two in order to give the average stock figure for the period.

For example: Jan. 1.   Stock   £6000

Dec. 31.   Stock   £4000
£10 000

Average stock equals   £10 000 = £5000
2

Sales at cost price can be calculated by deducting the percentage *gross profit* margin from the turnover figure. For example, if sales amount to £18 000 and gross profit is 33⅓ % of sales, then the cost of sales is worked out as follows:

Sales	£18 000
Less gross profit	6 000
Cost of sales	£12 000

Alternatively, the rate of turnover can be calculated by dividing the average *stock at selling price* into the value of sales. (Stock valued at selling price can be calculated by adding on the percentage gross profit margin to the value of stock.)

For example, if the value of stock amounts to £36 000 and the gross profit margin is 33⅓%, then stock at selling price is worked out as follows:

Average stock	£36 000
Gross profit	12 000
Average stock at selling price	£48 000

Thus:

$$\text{Rate of turnover} = \frac{\text{Sales}}{\text{Average stock at selling price}}$$

It is important to remember that the rate of stockturn will be calculated incorrectly if the cost and sales figures are confused. For example, the average stock at cost price must not be divided into a turnover figure based on selling price.

Disadvantages of a slow rate of turnover

Some commodities, such as greengrocery and fish, are perishable and unless sold within a few days they lose their freshness and may waste. If this happens the trader suffers financial loss.

- The longer that goods remain in stock the greater is the risk of damage due to careless handling. If deterioration does occur, goods will have to be sold at reduced prices with a consequent loss of profit to the trader.
- Some goods, such as clothes and footwear, may go out of fashion if they remain unsold at the end of the season. A trader will try, therefore, to sell off these kinds of goods by holding an end-of-season sale. Again some loss of profit due to reduced prices will be incurred.

Benefits of a fast rate of turnover

Clearly there are benefits to be gained by attempting to speed up the rate of stockturn.

- A trader with a fast rate of stockturn can buy in the most up-to-date goods and this is important when fashions change or manufacturers produce new models, as is the case, for example, with clothes, footwear, cars, television sets and many other kinds of consumer goods.
- A trader with a fast rate of stockturn requires less capital than a competitor who turns stock over more slowly. For example, one trader may buy £1000 worth of stock which is sold by the end of six months. Another trader may buy £500 worth of stock every three months, selling each lot in the period in which it was bought. Both traders sell the same amount in a year, but the first trader's initial investment in stock amount to £1000, while the second spends only £500. Thus the second trader needs less capital than the trader with the slower rate of turnover.
- An increase in stockturn will lead to an increase in turnover as can be seen from the following:

$$\frac{\text{Value of average stock}}{\text{at selling price}} \times \text{rate of turnover} = \text{turnover}.$$

An increase in sales normally also leads to an increase in profit if the trader has correctly balanced up the various factors.

Increasing the rate of turnover

A trader can increase the rate of turnover in a variety of ways.

By cutting prices
A policy of cutting prices in order to increase sales is known sometimes as the principle of 'small profits, quick returns'. For example, if 1000 articles can be sold at a profit of 30p each, there is a total profit of £300. If the price is reduced by 5p per article so that the profit on each article is only 25p, the trader must sell 1200 in order to make the same profit as before. However, if sales increase, as a result of the price reduction, to over 1200, then the cut in price will be justified. For example, if 1300 articles were sold the profit would be £325 compared with £300 profit made at the higher price. Fixing the right balance between price reductions in order to increase the rate of turnover, and the proportion of extra sales in order to increase overall profits is a matter requiring sound judgement. If, for example, the selling price is reduced by too big a margin, profits may well decline.

By increasing the amount of advertising
The various methods of advertising are considered in Chapter 17. The purpose of an advertising campaign is to attract more customers and so increase the rate of turnover.

By offering sales on credit
Another method of increasing the rate of turnover is for the trader to offer credit in addition to selling for cash. By doing so the trader hopes to gain some custom from those who cannot afford to pay the full cash price at once.

By improving stock
Yet again, the trader could increase the choice of brands offered to customers from stock; or different lines of goods could be introduced in order to attract additional custom.

11.3   Profit

Profit is the reward of enterprise. It is the surplus that remains when the total costs incurred by a business in a particular period (e.g. one year) are deducted from the income for that period.

Profits are either gross or net.

The *gross profit* is the excess of sales over the cost price of the goods sold. For example, if an article is bought for £1 and sold for £1.50 then the gross profit is 50p.

When a business firm draws up accounts at the end of its financial year, the first account is the *trading account* and its purpose is to calculate the gross profit or loss on trading.

If all the goods bought by a business were sold by the end of the year, the gross profit could be found by deducting the purchases from the sales. However some goods will be unsold at the end of the year and it is necessary then to work out the cost of the goods sold. In order to do this, the trader *takes stock* and calculates the cost of goods unsold at the end of the year. By deducting the value of stock from the total purchases plus stock in hand at the beginning of the year, the trader arrives at the cost price of goods sold.

Fig. 11.3   *A trading account*

Trading Account for the year ending 31 December 19—		
	£	£
Sales		15 660
Less cost of goods sold:		
Stock of goods		
1 January	1 080	
Plus Purchases	10 920	
	12 000	
Less Stock of goods:		
31 December	1 760	10 240
Gross Profit		£5 420

The trading account shows that when the trader valued stock at the end of the previous year it came to £1080. During the year additional stock was bought to the value of £10 920. At the end of the year, the trader took stock again and valued it at £1760

During the year total sales came to £15 660. The cost of goods sold amounted to £10 240 and the gross profit was £5420. If the cost of goods sold had been higher than the value of sales then the difference would have indicated a *gross loss*.

Mark up

The gross profit on a single article is sometimes called *mark up*. Thus a retailer who buys an article at a cost of 50p may mark up the article to sell at 60p. The mark up or gross profit is then 10p. Mark up is often expressed as a percentage of either cost price or selling price. For example:

$$\frac{10p}{50} \times 100 = 20 \text{ per cent on cost price}$$

$$\frac{10p}{60} \times 100 = 16.66 \text{ per cent on selling price}$$

The *net profit* is the balance remaining after all business expenses have been deducted from the gross profit. It is calculated in the *profit and loss account*. The expenses of running a business, such as payments for rent, rates, wages and advertising are called *overhead costs* or *working expenses*. The owner of a business is interested mainly in the net profit because this represents the reward for enterprise.

Fig. 11.4   *Profit and loss account*

Profit and Loss Account for the year ending 31 December 19 –		
	£	£
Gross profit		5240
Less expenses:		
Rent and Rates	700	
Stationery	532	
Salaries	1700	
Light and heat	100	3032
Net profit		£2388

This account shows that the working expenses of the business came to £3032. The gross profit figure for the same period is £5420 and the difference between the two totals (£2388) represents the net profit for the year. If the total expenses exceed the gross profit, then the difference indicates a *net loss*.

Comparison of profits

A trader may wish to compare the current profit figure with those of previous years. Alternatively a comparison may be required between the results of two separate businesses. There are two ways of making this comparison; by examining either the *profitability of sales* or the *return on the capital employed*.

Sales

A straight comparison of profits expressed in money terms can be misleading because no account is taken of price changes or of the quantity of goods sold. It is wisest, to express the profits as a percentage of the sales turnover.

Example:

	Year 1	*Year 2*
Turnover	£20 000	£30 000
Gross profit	5000	6000
Net profit	3000	3900

A comparison of the *gross profit* figures indicates that Year 2 was a more profitable year. However, when the gross profit figures are expressed as a percentage of the turnover, the results are as follows:

Year 1

$$\frac{\text{Gross profit}}{\text{Turnover}} \times 100 = \frac{5000}{20\ 000} \times 100 = 25\%$$

Year 2

$$\frac{6000}{30\ 000} \times 100 = 20\%$$

These percentages mean that for every £100 worth of goods sold in Year 1, the trader made £25 gross profit. In Year 2 this figure fell to £20. Thus the profitability of the business actually declined in Year 2, contrary to the impression created by a straight comparison of the gross profit figures.

When the gross profit percentage declines, it may be an indication that the cost of buying stock has risen. The trader may do better by a change of supplier. Alternatively, selling prices may have to be raised.

A comparison between the *net profit* figures expressed as a percentage of the turnover shows the following:

Year 1

$$\frac{\text{Net profit}}{\text{Turnover}} \times 100 = \frac{3000}{20\,000} \times 100 = 15\%$$

Year 2

$$\frac{3900}{30\,000} \times 100 = 13\%$$

Thus for every £100 worth of goods sold in Year 1, the trader received £15 net profit whereas in Year 2 only £13 was received for every £100 worth of goods sold.

These two lots of calculations taken together also indicate that in Year 2 the trader had to pay £87 in order to make £13 clear profit. The cost of the goods sold accounted for £80, and £7 represented the overhead expenses of the business. In Year 1 the cost of the goods sold was £75 and the overhead expenses account for £10. A large increase in expenses indicates a need for greater efficiency in controlling the overheads of the business.

With capital
The larger the amount of capital invested in a business, the greater will be the profits expected from it. In order to discover the percentage return of profit on capital, the trader will use the following formula:

$$\frac{\text{Net profit}}{\text{Capital}} \times 100$$

If it is assumed that the trader's capital was £15000, then the percentage of net profit to capital is as follows:

Year 1

$$\frac{3000}{15\,000} \times 100 = 20\%$$

Year 2

$$\frac{3900}{15\ 000} \times 100 = 26\%$$

Thus, in Year 1 the trader earned £20 for every £100 invested in the business, and £26 was earned in Year 2. These are reasonable returns on the capital invested.

If the returns were less than 10% the business would be judged to be a poor investment. The trader might have been wiser to lend money to the government or to a building society, and earn up to 10% without risk or worry. Capital invested in a business is expected to earn more than the rate of interest paid by 'safe borrowers' for loans. If it does not do so, there is little point in investing capital in the business.

11.4   Costs

The total costs of a business consist of fixed costs and variable costs.

Fixed costs
These are the costs which have to be paid whether a trader sells a large or a small quantity of goods. For example, if a retailer pays rent for shop premises, the amount has to be paid regardless of the amount of the weekly takings. Similarly, if a salaried assistant is employed, the amount of the salary will have to be paid however many customers come into the shop. Other examples of fixed costs are rates, cleaning, interest payments on loans and lighting bills.

Variable costs
These costs change when the volume of sales changes. Usually variable costs increase or decrease with the sales. For example, if more goods are sold, the cost of wages, delivery, postage and cash discount may also rise. On the other hand, if fewer goods are sold, these expenses may decline.

Average cost
This is a term which refers to the average cost of producing or selling a single article. It consists of average fixed costs and average variable costs. When sales are small, average cost will be

high because the fixed costs will be spread over a small number of articles. As sales increase, average cost will fall because the fixed costs are being distributed over a larger number of articles.

Costs and turnover

A trader will keep a careful watch on the overhead expenses of the business because a rise in their total reduces the net profit. In order to compare working expenses with previous years, the various items may be calculated as percentages of the turnover of the business. Alternatively the *total* of working expenses can be expressed as a percentage of turnover. For example, if working expenses amount to £1000 and turnover is £8000 then the calculation is as follows:

$$\frac{\text{Working expenses}}{\text{Turnover}} \times 100 = \frac{1000}{8000} \times 100 = 12.5\%$$

Thus the working expenses amount to £12.50 for every £100 worth of goods sold. The trader will obviously try to keep this percentage as low as possible.

Test Yourself

1 Money invested in a business is called _____.
2 Why might the capital employed in a business differ from the figure for capital owned?
3 Premises and machinery are examples of _____ capital.
4 Cash, raw materials and stocks of goods are examples of _____ capital.
5 Why does a business need working capital?
6 How is working capital calculated?
7 List the drawbacks to a trader of a lack of working capital.
8 What is the meaning of 'overtrading'?
9 In what ways can a shortage of working capital be remedied?
10 Why does a manufacturer have a larger proportion of fixed capital than either a retailer or a wholesaler?
11 What is turnover?
12 The number of times the average stock is sold during a year is called _____.
13 Write down the formula for calculating the rate of turnover.
14 What are the disadvantages of a slow rate of turnover?

15 What are the benefits of a fast rate of turnover?
16 Name the various ways by which a trader can increase the rate of turnover.
17 The difference between cost price and selling price is called _____.
18 How does net profit differ from gross profit?
19 The expenses of running a business are called _____
20 Explain what the following mean:
    (*a*) gross profit is 30% of turnover
    (*b*) net profit is 20% of turnover.
21 Why would a trader consider that a net profit return of 5% on capital was unsatisfactory?
22 What is the difference between fixed and variable costs?
23 What is average cost?
24 Why do average costs fall as sales increase?

Chapter 12

Exports and Imports

12.1 International Trade

Trade between countries differs from trade within a country in a number of ways.

Language
Different countries have different languages and this can be a barrier to trade. Traders who sell abroad may have to employ language specialists and incur additional expense through the necessity of having special forms, labels, instructions, etc. printed.

Currency
Each country has a different currency: that is, a different type of money which is acceptable only within its own frontiers. In Britain the currency is the pound sterling, in France the franc, while in the United States the dollar is used. If a British importer buys goods from a French manufacturer, then payment must be made in francs which have to be purchased in the *foreign exchange market*. Such a procedure is more costly and time-consuming than payment in the home trade. Furthermore foreign exchange rates vary and an adverse movement in the conversion rate may involve a trader in a loss.

Payment
Payment for international sales may be longer delayed and less certain than payment for home sales. An exporter has to obtain payment from a debtor who may live on the other side of the world. The exporter will be reluctant to ship the goods without being reasonably certain of payment, while the importer will not wish to pay without some guarantee of receipt of the goods.

Distance
The risks involved in transporting goods increase with the distance and the number of times the goods are handled. Hence there is greater likelihood of loss, damage or delay when sending goods to countries abroad.

Customs duties and import quotas
Certain goods may be subject to heavy *duties* or *tariffs*, making it almost impossible for exports to compete in price with home production. In addition, exports may be limited by *quotas* imposed by importing countries.

Even if exporters consider they can compete (in spite of customs duties) it is necessary to ensure that the correct duty is paid. Duties vary according to the way that goods are classified. Thus the duty may be assessed at a certain percentage of the price of the goods, as for example, 15% on vehicles (when it is said to be an *ad valorem duty*), or it may be charged on the quantity or weight of the commodities, as for example, 5p per litre on oil, (when it is termed a *specific duty*). Hence a correct understanding of the classifications list is essential.

Finally, an exporter runs the risk that duties and quotas may be changed suddenly so that the market in a particular country may shrink or even vanish overnight.

Competition
At home a manufacturer may be sheltered from foreign competition by duties or quotas imposed by the home government. Hence competition may be restricted to other home manufacturers. However, in overseas markets, the manufacturer may have to face competition from producers in that market and from other foreign exporters.

Local conditions
An exporter has to consider the customs and habits of the countries to which goods are sold. For example, foreign customers may like their goods in different dimensions and in different kinds of packages from those found suitable in the home market. Similarly, attention must be given to the methods of trading adopted in foreign markets. For example, at home, manufacturers may leave the provision of spare parts and an after-sales service to others, but if no such facilities are available abroad they must make some provision for this themselves.

Thus trading abroad involves considerably greater risks and difficulties than the home trade. A producer who intends to prepare goods for new foreign markets will be wise to undertake marke research, the object of which is to secure information to help in formulating selling policies. Thus the buying habits of consumers, the extent of competitors' sales, and the trend of sales over a given period of time provide important relevant statistics. Market research is also used to discover why consumers purchase the goods they do; to study ways of packaging goods so as to make them attractive to the consumer; and to make sales forecasts.

Advantages of international trade

The main benefits derived from trade between countries are outlined below.

Variety
Without international trade, many countries would have to go without some products. For example, countries with a temperate climate would have to do without cotton, rice and certain fruits; others would be unable to use minerals which were unobtainable at home. Thus international trade enables each country to enjoy a variety of products.

Efficiency
Access to an enlarged international market enables industries to attain greater productivity. Selling abroad as well as at home extends the market and so makes increased output possible.

Specialisation
Foreign trade enables each country to specialise in the production of those commodities for which it it most fitted by natural conditions – climate, soil, etc. In addition, the peoples of the world differ in talents and abilities. The differences may be in skills which have been acquired by tradition (e.g. wine-making in certain parts of France, Italy and Portugal) or those taught through education and training (e.g. engineering). Thus foreign trade permits a country to concentrate on producing those goods and services for which its resources are most suited and at the same time, to satisfy its other wants by importing.

Interdependence
International trade makes the countries of the world inter-dependent. A country depends upon others (*a*) for supplying its deficiencies in goods and services and (*b*) for markets for its own products. Trade may lead to an exchange of knowledge and culture between countries which, it has been argued, should reduce the possibility of war.

Services

In addition to trading in *goods*, countries perform *services* for one another. Goods are usually referred to as *visible* items because they can be seen and recognised. Services are termed *invisible* items because they cannot be seen or touched. Those services which are sold to people in overseas countries are invisible exports while services bought by people in the home country are invisible imports. As with visible items, payment is made abroad for imports and money is received for exports. The nature of invisible imports and exports is summarised in Figure 12.1.

The item showing receipts for *other private services* includes the earnings of the City of London for the provision of insurance, banking and other financial services for overseas customers. Under this heading are also included the royalties received from the sale of books and records overseas.

12.2   Exports

Orders for exports are obtained in various ways.

1 Many firms send representatives abroad to obtain orders from new customers and to maintain existing accounts.
2 Representatives of foreign firms may visit this country to make purchases.
3 A number of countries hold trade fairs and exhibitions. Buyers and sellers attend from different countries, and firms exhibit their goods. In the UK, fairs such as the Motor Show and the Boat Show attract buyers from both home and overseas.
4 Orders from abroad may be obtained by advertising in trade journals and sending circulars and catalogues to selected firms.
5 In addition to orders received direct from foreign importers, British manufacturers also receive export orders from export merchants and commission agents. An *export merchant* buys from home manufacturers and sells both at home and abroad (see page 52). A *commission agent*, on the other hand, acts on behalf of a principal abroad. The agent places the order with a British manufacturer and makes suitable arrangements for the packing and shipment of the goods.

A foreign order is often called an *indent* and an order received from a foreign buyer by a commission agent may be either a *closed indent* or an *open indent*. A closed indent instructs the agent to order goods only from a certain firm; an open indent instructs the agent to orders goods but no particular firm is specified.

Fig. 12.1 *Invisible imports and exports*

Payments (Invisible imports)	*Receipts* (Invisible exports)
Government Expenditure on government services abroad, e.g. cost of keeping troops abroad, cost of embassies and diplomatic expenses.	Payments by foreign governments for their forces and diplomatic services in the UK.
Transport Charges made by foreign shipping companies and airlines for carriage of British people and goods.	Earnings of UK shipping and airlines through carrying foreign people and goods.
Travel Spending by British tourists and business people abroad.	Money spent by overseas visitors in the UK.
Interest, profit and dividends Payments made to foreign owners and lenders of capital by firms in the UK.	Income received from overseas investments held by private people and firms, and by the British government.
Private transfers Money sent (e.g. gifts, pensions) by people in the UK to relatives and friends abroad.	Money sent by people abroad to residents in the UK.
Government transfers Economic grants to developing countries made directly or through international organisations.	Economic grants received from foreign governments and organisations.
Other private services Payments made to foreign firms for various financial and other services.	Earnings received for financial and other services to foreign firms.

Government assistance to exporters

The government assists businesses to sell abroad in a number of ways.

Exporters who apply to the *Department of Trade and Industry* for information and advice will be told the prospects for exports in any country in the world. The Department will also advise on import regulations and customs duties; provide details of particular markets; and report on the commercial standing of firms wishing to import British goods.

The Department encourages exports by publicising information about exhibitions and trade fairs both in this country and abroad. It also organises British Weeks in overseas countries as advertisements for UK exports.

Acting with the approval of Parliament, the Department has made trade agreements with foreign countries. Usually such agreements include arrangements whereby each country agrees to buy certain quantities of each other's goods, every year.

In essence, the Department seeks to increase exports by providing assistance without interference.

The *Export Credits Guarantee Department* (*ECGD*) of the Department of Trade assists exporters by undertaking insurance against the non-payment of debts by foreign import merchants. The risks covered are of two kinds – commercial and political.

Commercial risks include the insolvency of the buyer and any other cause of loss occurring outside the UK, beyond the control of the traders concerned, and not normally insurable with insurance companies. *Political risks* include a declaration of war between Britain and the importer's country, and the imposition of import restrictions by an overseas government.

In addition to providing cover for credit risks on overseas buyers as outlined above, the ECGD provides financial guarantees which enable exporters to give long-term export credit finance, and to borrow from their banks against their ultimate receipts.

Chambers of commerce

Advice on foreign markets is available from chambers of commerce.

Almost every industrial town has a local association of the principal industrial and commercial firms called a *chamber of commerce*. Its main purpose is to promote home and foreign trade, and in particular, the trade of the district in which the chamber of commerce is established. The interests of the local chambers of commerce are represented nationally by the Association of British Chambers of Commerce, while the International Chamber of Commerce represents commerce chambers in many countries.

Chambers of commerce collect information on all subjects likely to be of interest to their members. Consequently, advice and information is available to members on such matters as trade and industry in any country; customs duties and regulations; translation of letters and documents; agents and collection of debts in countries abroad.

In addition to providing services for exporters, chambers of commerce perform other functions, including analysing problems affecting trade in the towns and districts in which they are situated; and advancing education and training for industry and commerce.

Chambers of commerce should not be confused with *chambers of trade* or *trade associations*. The former are more local in character and are composed mostly of retailers who meet periodically to discuss any topic which affects trade (for example, hours of business, car parking facilities, and other matters which might prove inconvenient to customers and so affect trade). Trade associations, on the other hand, are formed by traders in the same line of business. Examples are the Society of Motor Manufacturers and Traders, and the Electric Lamp Manufacturers' Association. These associations give their members similar services to chambers of commerce, but in relation to one particular industry or trade.

Export documents

The treatment of export documents remains one of the more complicated aspects of overseas trade. Assistance in eliminating difficulties is available from (*i*) the major banks who have specialist staff capable of providing information on documentary queries; (*ii*) the Department of Trade and Industry which offers extensive guidance through its Export Services Division, (*iii*) HM Customs and Excise, (*iv*) chambers of commerce.

Despite the availability of sources of assistance, some firms – for one reason or another, such as lack of knowledge, experience or staff – prefer to employ others to do the work. For example, an exporter may sell goods to an *export merchant house* which will arrange for documentation, shipment and collection of payment from the overseas buyer. Where a manufacturer prefers to export direct, it may be helpful to employ a *freight and forwarding agent* who will, in return for a commission, take over packing, documentation, insurance, etc.

Export licence

Before undertaking any sales abroad an exporter must discover whether or not an export licence from the Department of Trade is needed. At present few goods require export licences. Exceptions are scrap metals, goods of military or strategic importance, and works of art that amount to national treasures.

Invoice
This document is a summary of a sale of goods and is sent by the seller to the buyer.

Insurance documents
The terms of the contract determine whether the seller or the buyer should insure the goods while in transit. For example, an exporter who has quoted *c.i.f* terms (cost, insurance, freight) has to insure the goods for the sea journey. The *insurance certificate* is evidence that insurance has been taken out.

Certificates of origin
These are sometimes required (*a*) by the governments in importing countries in order to certify that the goods originate from a country from which imports are permitted, (*b*) by the importer to support a claim for preferential import duty. The regulations of the importing country may determine whether the certification as to origin needs to be made by the exporter only, or by a chamber of commerce, or by the diplomatic representative in the UK of the country concerned.

Where a certificate of origin is required to be issued by an official body this may be done in the UK solely by approved chambers of commerce, acting under the authority of the Department of Trade. Where the declaration of origin has to be made by an official representative of the importing country, then this may take the form of either a *commercial invoice* certified by the consulate, or a special invoice obtained from the consul and called a *consular invoice*.

Bill of lading
This is an important document used in the shipping of goods. It is made out by the exporter of the goods and gives details of the goods and their destination. The exporter retains one copy of the bill, another is kept by the master of the vessel and a third is dispatched to the importer. Since the bill of lading is a *document of title* (which means that whoever holds the bill has the right to legal ownership of the goods), it is very important that the importer should receive a copy before the shipment arrives. Upon the arrival of the ship the importer must present the bill of lading in order the claim the goods. Since the bill is transferable

by *endorsement* a consignment of goods can be sold before their arrival at the port by the endorsement of the bill by the importer.

When goods are taken on board ship they are checked by *tally clerks*. If faults are found in the goods or in their packing, a note is made to this effect on the bill and the latter is then known as a *dirty bill*. The purpose of recording these defects is to safeguard the ship-owner against claims for damage. A bill without any notes is known as a *clean bill*.

In addition to being a document of title, a bill serves (*a*) as an acknowledgement of the *receipt* of goods by the ship-owner and (*b*) as a *contract of carriage* between the exporter of the goods and the ship-owner.

The transport of goods in containers is a development which has led in many cases to the replacement of traditional bills of lading by combined transport documents, often referred to as *container bills of lading*. These documents may cover the carriage of goods from port to port or transit from an inland point of departure to an inland point of destination, which may include an intermediate sea passage.

Other documents
- Air consignment notes (*air waybills*) and *parcel post receipts* serve as receipts for the goods and as evidence of dispatch to the importer.
- A *mate's receipt* is a temporary receipt for the goods given by or on behalf of the ship's master, acknowledging that the goods are on board, pending issue of the bills of lading.
- A *shipping note* is a formal request to the port authority to receive the goods specified. It accompanies the goods to the dock, setting out the details of the ship, the dock, and the goods.
- Details of all exports must be given to the *customs* authorities on documents called *specification forms*. The information supplied includes the quantity and *f.o.b.* (free on board) value of the goods exported and the country to which they have been dispatched. The information is used by the customs authorities to compile the monthly *export statistics*.

Export documentation within the European Community

Trade between member countries of the *European Community* is conducted under the *Community Transit System*. The procedure is as follows. A declaration is filled in by the exporter, or the exporter's agent, and countersigned by the Customs Office of Departure. Copies of the form bearing the declaration travel with the goods and are thus available for inspection by customs officials at each frontier, where a *transit advice note* is also deposited giving particulars of the journey. On arrival at the Customs Office of Destination, the certified declaration is presented with the goods. One copy is receipted and mailed to the Customs Office of Departure. This method satisfies the Office of Departure that the goods have left its national territory and, correspondingly, the Office of Destination is satisfied that the goods have arrived intact. The intermediate countries in their turn, have seen the declaration, and know that the Customs Offices at the start and finish of the journey will see that all the goods advised are accounted for.

Export merchants

Exporting is a difficult business involving a great deal of work and detailed knowledge about goods, markets, packing, transport and the commercial law of other countries. Because of these problems many manufacturers prefer not to undertake exporting themselves. Instead they deal with export merchants. The latter are in business on their own account and specialise in certain overseas markets. A manufacturer sells goods to them and is paid promptly in the same way as when sales are made to wholesalers in the home trade. Thus the manufacturer is relieved of many of the tasks and financial problems associated with exporting.

The merchant has an expert knowledge of export procedure, and dealing in goods supplied by many makers means that expenses can be spread over a large turnover. It may be cheaper for the manufacturers, particularly the smaller ones, to use export merchants instead of setting up their own exporting departments. Certainly, without their help and advice many small-scale exporters might not enter the export market at all.

12.3   Imports

Taxes known as *customs duties* or *tariffs* have to be paid on many goods imported from abroad. The purpose of customs duties is to:

- protect home manufacturers against foreign competition by raising the price of the imported article;
- raise revenue through the taxation system.

Whether goods are liable to duty or not, certain forms must be filled in by the importer and handed to customs officials. These forms or *entries* provide full particulars of the goods, and form the basis for the official figures of total imports.

If no duty is payable, the importer completes a form called *entry for free goods*. A form known as *entry for home use* is filled in when dutiable goods are required for immediate use. As soon as the importer pays the duty the goods are released by the customs officials. However, if the importer intends to store dutiable goods in a bonded warehouse, the customs form is called an *entry for warehousing*.

Bonded warehouses

If the importer does not wish to pay the duty on dutiable goods at once, the goods may be stored in a bonded warehouse. The warehouse acknowledges the receiving of the goods by issuing a *warehouse warrant* to the importer. A warehouse warrant is a document of title and it can be endorsed and passed on if the goods are sold while in the warehouse. The warrant must be produced before the goods can be removed from the warehouse.

Bonded warehouses exist at the principal ports, and goods subject to duty cannot be removed from them until the duty has been paid. While stored in the bonded warehouse, the goods can be prepared for sale (for example, wines may be bottled and packed) and prospective buyers can inspect the goods. The word 'bonded' is used to describe this kind of warehouse because the owner has signed a *bond* (or pledge) with the customs authorities to the effect that goods will not be removed from the warehouse until the duty has been paid.

If goods on which duty has been paid are *re-exported* to foreign countries, the money is refunded by the customs. The repayment is known as a *customs drawback*.

12.4 Balance of Trade

The customs authorities provide the Department of Trade and Industry with details of goods entering and leaving the UK.

Exports are valued free on board (*f.o.b.*) which means that payment received by the exporter includes only the carriage charge as far as the ship. Additional transport and insurance costs incurred in getting the goods to their destination are paid by the importer. Imports to the UK are shown as including cost, insurance and freight (*c.i.f.*). Hence the trade statistics tend to overvalue the total amount spent on imports.

From the information supplied by the customs authorities, the Department produces a monthly statement giving a summary of imports and exports for the preceding month.

The *balance of trade* is the difference between the value of imports and exports (visible items only) for a particular year. When visible exports are higher than visible imports the balance of trade is said to be *favourable* – because sales exceed purchases. On the other hand, when imports exceed exports, the balance is *adverse* or *unfavourable*. Sometimes the latter situation is referred to as the *trade gap*.

12.5   Balance of Payments

The annual statement of all payments made to countries and total receipts from them is known as the *balance of payments*.

Current account

The current account comprises money for current dealings as opposed to money for investment. It is made up of two parts, namely visible trade and invisible trade (see Figure 12.2).

Fig. 12.2   *Balance of payments current account (£m)*

	Visible Account			Invisible Account balance	Current Account Balance
	Exports	Imports	Balance of Trade		
Year 1	28987	25416	−3571	+2344	−1227
Year 2	33973	36780	+2807	+2015	+4822

The *current balance* (i.e. the balance of visible and invisible trade taken together) shows whether the country is making a profit or loss on day-to-day dealings. Thus a surplus over a number of years demonstrates that sufficient foreign currency is being earned to buy imports and to build up reserves of foreign currency.

Capital flows

Apart from the current account, there are other flows of money into or out of the country: these are *flows of capital*. They comprise, for example, money going out of Britain for investment in industry or property, and money coming into Britain for similar purposes; loans between the British government and other governments; borrowing abroad by the nationalised industries and local authorities; credit given for exports and received when buying imports. Other flows are provided by overseas countries, and their private citizens and firms, adding to or withdrawing from the bank balances they hold in the UK; and the lending and other dealings in foreign currencies of UK banks.

When the total of these *capital transactions* is added to the current balance, it never tallies exactly with the amount of foreign currency which the country has in fact gained or lost in the year (this amount is recorded exactly by the Bank of England). Few of the transactions in the accounts can be recorded precisely – for example, the foreign spending of British people taking holidays abroad, or money spent by tourists in the UK. An additional difficulty is the difference of timing between transactions and payments. For example, exports may be shipped abroad in December and the payments for them come in in the following March, so that some payments relating to the year ending in December will be incorporated in the next year's figures for the total currency flow. Thus variation in timing from year to year makes consistent recording impossible. The *balancing item* – in effect the total of recording errors and omissions – makes up the difference between the total value of the transactions recorded and the precise accounts kept by the Bank of England. If the balancing item is *plus*, it means that more money has actually come in than the records of transactions have shown. If it is *minus*, the opposite is the case.

Total currency flow

When added together, the current balance plus the total of

capital flows plus the balancing item give the total currency flow which has come into (*plus*) or gone out of (*minus*) the country.

If the flow is a plus figure, it shows the money available for (*a*) adding to the foreign exchange reserves or (*b*) repaying loans from overseas. When there is a loss – a minus currency outflow – it has to be covered by (*a*) drawing on the foreign currency reserves or (*b*) borrowing from overseas central banks or (*c*) borrowing from the *International Monetary Fund* (*IMF*). The IMF is a fund of currencies contributed by the member countries and it provides short-term borrowing facilities for countries in temporary balance of payments difficulties. There are two further ways of covering a loss: foreign investments can be sold to raise funds, or bank deposits from abroad can be attracted into the country by high interest rates.

However, each of these methods possesses a disadvantage in that it will create future difficulties: loans have to be repaid, generally with interest; the IMF imposes certain conditions on borrowers (with the aim of helping them to solve their problems); the sale of foreign investments reduces future income; while bank deposits are very volatile and can be quickly moved to another country with higher interest rates (hence the term 'hot money').

Official financing

The last two rows of figures in Figure 12.3 show how the government has covered a net loss or used a net gain. The plus and minus signs may appear rather confusing because plus is usually taken as favourable and minus as unfavourable, as is the case in the current account. In fact, the minus sign here means money going 'out' to pay off debts or into the reserves, and is therefore a good indication; whereas a plus means additional government borrowing from abroad or 'borrowing' from the reserves, both of which are unfavourable.

Summary

The two totals in the annual statement which are of most importance are:

● the current balance – showing the country's position in day-to-day dealings with the rest of the world;

	Year 1	Year 2	Year 3	Year 4	Year 5	Year 6	Year 7	Year 8	Year 9	Year 10	Year 11
Current account											
Visible trade	−223	−66	−554	−667	−156	−25	+280	−702	−2334	−5520	−3204
Invisibles	+197	+167	+256	+395	+616	+758	+804	+856	+1598	+1873	+1531
Current balance	−26	+101	−298	−272	+460	+733	+1084	+154	−736	−3347	−1673
Current balance	−26	+101	−298	−272	+460	+733	+1084	+154	−736	−3347	−1673
Capital transfers	—	—	—	—	—	—	—	—	−59	−75	—
Investment and other capital flows	−326	−578	−600	−1006	−165	+573	+1817	−714	−39	+1614	+188
Balancing item	−1	−70	−227	−132	+392	−19	+245	−705	+45	+136	+6
Balance for official financing	−353	−547	−671	−1410	+687	+1287	+3146	−1265	−789	−1672	−1479
Allocation of Special Drawing Rights (+)	—	—	—	—	—	+171	+125	+124	—	—	—
Gold subscription to IMF (−)	—	−44	—	—	—	−38	—	—	—	—	—
Official financing											
Net transactions with overseas monetary authorities	+599	+625	+556	+1296	−699	−1295	−1817	+449	—	—	—
Foreign currency borrowing: by HM Government	—	—	—	—	—	—	—	—	—	+644	+423
by public sector under exchange cover schemes	—	—	—	—	+56	—	+82	—	+999	+1107	+387
Official reserves (drawings on +/additions to −)	−246	−34	+115	+114	−44	−125	−1536	+692	−210	−79	+669

Note: Special Drawing Rights refers to a facility available to member countries of the International Monetary Fund (IMF). In some years there is also a gold subscription to the IMF.
Source: *United Kingdom Balance of Payments*

- the total currency flow – showing the country's ability or inability to build up reserves or pay off debts.

12.6   Foreign Exchange

One of the problems associated with international trade is that each country has its own kind of money which is generally unacceptable in another country. For example, the Spanish peseta is of no use to a UK exporter who has sold cars to a Spanish importer unless (*a*) the exporter wants to buy Spanish goods with the pesetas or (*b*) the pesetas can be exchanged for pounds sterling. Alternatively, the UK exporter may receive payment in sterling, in which case the buyer must obtain pounds with Spanish currency.

Thus when international trade takes place an *exchange of currencies* is necessary. In practice, this work is performed by the banks on behalf of their customers. Figure 12.4 explains the process. The *foreign exchange market* consists of most banks together with a small number of firms who specialise as *foreign exchange brokers*. There is no meeting place for the market since nearly all business is conducted over the telephone and via telex or other data transmission systems. Banks throughout the world conduct business with each other in this way and the market is, therefore, international. Through the foreign exchange market, each currency acquires a value in terms of the other currencies which can be bought and sold for it.

An *exchange rate* is the price of one currency in terms of another. It is determined mainly by the supply of, and demand for, the particular currency. The supply of pounds, for example, depends on the extent to which people, businesses and governments wish to sell pounds in exchange for other currencies. The

Fig. 12.4   *International payment*

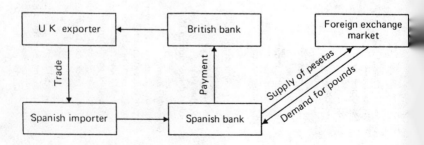

sellers will include UK importers and investors in foreign firms. On the other hand, those who create the demand for pounds will include foreign importers and overseas investors in British government stocks and the shares of UK companies.

The foreign currency earned by UK firms through exporting is held by the banks and forms part of the country's *foreign currency reserves*. If earnings from exports are less than the amount spent on imports, then British banks will have been selling more pounds to get foreign currency than foreign banks will have wanted to buy for their own importers. The extra pounds will have been bought by the Bank of England in exchange for part of the foreign currency reserves built up in previous years.

If the reserves were in danger of being used up, the Bank of England would have to borrow foreign currency from other central banks. Thus, it is essential that the export earnings of British firms are sufficient to provide importers with the currency they need. Hence the importance of the balance of payments current account which shows whether or not Britain is paying her way in world trade.

12.7 Trade Barriers

Governments place restrictions on imports for several reasons. In the first place, duties may be imposed in order to raise revenue through the taxation system. Secondly, a government may wish to protect home manufacturers against foreign competition by raising the prices of imported goods. Finally, restrictions on imports may be considered necessary if there is a deficit in the balance of payments current account.

Imports may be limited by tariffs, quotas, exchange control and subsidies.

Tariffs

Tariffs are taxes on foreign goods levied at the port of entry. They protect home industries by making foreign goods relatively more expensive in the home market.

Quotas

These place a physical limit on the quantities of goods that may be imported during a certain period (e.g. a country may impose an import quota of not more than 12 000 motor cars per year). This again protects home producers from foreign competition because buyers will be forced to purchase home-produced goods if imports are scarce.

Exchange control
Exchange control is a way of limiting the volume of imports by controlling the supply of foreign currencies made available to importers. Thus once an allotment of foreign currency has been spent, no more imports will be allowed during the remainder of the allotment period.

Subsidies
Whereas tariffs make foreign goods more expensive in the home market, *subsidies* make home-produced goods cheaper in the home market. This financial assistance to home producers is a method of protection against foreign competition.

12.8   Free Trade

During the years since the end of the Second World War (1939-45) there has been considerable growth in the volume of world trade. An important contribution to this development has been made by international organisations set up to work for the removal of trade restrictions. *GATT* (*General Agreement on Tariffs and Trade*) is one of these organisations. It operates by holding periodic conferences of member countries to negotiate agreements for the reduction of tariffs, quotas and other barriers to trade. A basic principle of GATT is the *most favoured nation* clause. This states that any tariff reduction agreed between any member country and another country, whether or not a member, must be extended to all other members of GATT so that no nation will be most favoured. Membership now comprises most countries of the non-communist world. Since GATT became operational in 1948, the organisation has succeeded in bringing about a significant increase in free trade.

Whereas GATT works for free trade on a worldwide basis, some countries have joined together to set up regional *free trade blocs*. Examples exist in Africa, the Caribbean and Eastern Europe, but the most important example is the *European Community* (*EC*) known popularly as the *Common Market*. It was established in 1957 by the *Treaty of Rome*. There are, at present twelve countries in the Community: the United Kingdom, France, West Germany, Italy, Luxemburg, Holland, the Republic of Ireland, Denmark, Belgium, Greece, Spain and Portugal. The aim of the EC is to reduce all obstacles to free trade between member countries and to maintain a common tariff against the rest of the world. The hope is that such economic co-operation will pave the way for greater political co-operation.

Member countries follow their own economic and political policies, but policies decided by the *Council of Ministers* (representatives of member countries) are honoured. Member countries contribute to the Community's Budget which finances the policies agreed by the Council of Ministers. There is also a *European Parliament,* whose members are elected by voters in member countries, and which acts as a watchdog on the activities of the Council of Ministers. A *Commission* is responsible for seeing that approved policies are carried out by member governments.

Test Yourself

1 List the differences between home trade and foreign trade.
2 List four advantages of international trade.
3 Describe briefly the characteristics of Britain's (*a*) exports and (*b*) imports.
4 What are (*a*) visible and (*b*) invisible items in international trade?
5 Write down three examples of (*a*) invisible imports and (*b*) invisible exports.
6 Name the various ways by which British manufacturers may receive export orders.
7 List four ways in which the government assists exporters.
8 Briefly describe the differences between chambers of commerce, chambers of trade and trade associations.
9 What is the purpose of a certificate of origin?
10 List the functions of a bill of lading.
11 What is a shipping note?
12 Briefly describe the role of an export merchant.
13 What are the purposes of customs duties?
14 Why are imports sometimes stored in a bonded warehouse?
15 What is a customs drawback?
16 How are (*a*) exports and (*b*) imports valued by the customs authorities?
17 Define the balance of trade.
18 When is the balance of trade (*a*) favourable (*b*) adverse?
19 Name the main sections of the balance of payments statement.
20 What is the difference between the balance of trade and the balance of payments?
21 Which kinds of trade make up the current account?
22 What is the importance of the current account?
23 Write down three examples of capital flows.

24 Why is there a balancing item in the balance of payments statement?
25 Which items comprise the total currency flow?
26 What uses can be made of a gain from total currency flow?
27 In what ways can a loss on total currency flow be covered?
28 What does the section 'Official Financing' show in the balance of payments statement?
29 What is an exchange rate?
30 State three reasons why governments restrict imports.
31 Write down four ways of restricting imports.
32 How does GATT operate?
33 What is the 'most favoured nation' clause?
34 When was the Common Market established?
35 What is the purpose of the European Parliament?

PART II

THE AIDS TO TRADE

Chapter 13

Banks

In Britain banking began with the London goldsmiths, who, because of the nature of their business, had facilities for storing valuables. Their first banking function, therefore, was accepting *deposits* of cash from merchants who had no safe place in which to keep their money.

After a time the receipts for deposits began to be used as a *means of payment* by merchants. Eventually the early bankers issued bank notes.

A more advanced stage in the development of banking came when bankers began to *lend money*. The increasing use of bank notes meant that people no longer needed to draw out cash from the bankers, who found it safe, therefore, to lend out at interest some of the money deposited with them.

In this brief outline of the origin of banking, there can be seen the development of the three main functions of banks at the present day:

- repositories for cash;
- agents for payment;
- sources of loans.

Types of bank

There are, at present, five main types of bank in the UK. They are:

- commercial banks
- the central bank
- merchant banks
- savings banks
- Girobank.

13.1   Commercial Banks

Banks which undertake most kinds of banking business are generally known as *commercial banks* or sometimes by their older name of *joint-stock banks*. The four main independent groups are:

- Barclays
- National Westminster Bank
- Midland Bank
- Lloyds Bank

The major commercial banks are also called clearing banks, because they are members of the London Clearing House, where cheques are exchanged and debts settled (see page 169).

The commercial banks have three main functions. They provide:

- a safe way in which customers can hold their savings;
- loans to businesses and private persons;
- a means of making payments.

Deposits

Commercial bank deposits are a convenient way of holding savings. Deposits can be made in either a *current account* or a *deposit account*, or in both.

Current accounts

A person who leaves money in a current account does not usually receive any interest from the bank (though there are exceptions) and may have to pay charges for the work done by the bank in conducting the account.

On the other hand, a current account has two advantages: (*a*) money can be withdrawn on demand; (*b*) payments may be made by cheque.

The current account depositor receives a cheque book which is used both to make payments to others and to withdraw cash. Paying into a current account is done by entering the details on a paying-in slip and handing this together with the cheques, notes and coins, to the cashier. When the items have been checked, the cashier will stamp the paying-in slip and the counterfoil or duplicate and return the latter (which acts a receipt) to the customer. The slip provides the bank with the details necessary for recording the transaction.

Deposits accounts

The holder of a deposit account does not pay charges, and receives interest from the bank. Normally, seven days' notice of withdrawal must be given, but immediate withdrawals are possible if the account holder is prepared to forfeit seven days' interest on the amount withdrawn. Payments cannot be made from a deposit account by cheque. The bank provides a record of deposits and withdrawals.

The bank statement

The bank keeps a record of every payment made into, and every withdrawal out of a current account. These records are maintained to show the day-to-day balance. The bank issues an exact copy of this (the *bank statement*) at regular intervals. In addition a customer can have a statement sent on request. The entries on the statement can be checked against the entries on the cheque-book counterfoils and paying-in slips.

Making loans

A large number and a wide variety of customers borrow from the commercial banks. Most of the banks' lending is to businesses but substantial amounts are also lent to public authorities (local councils, government departments and nationalised industries) and to private customers.

Like other businesses, the banks operate with the aim of making a *profit*. Income is earned by investing and lending the money deposited with the bank. Banks receive additional income from charges made for certain services, but the greater part of a bank's earnings arises from lending and charging interest.

An important method of lending is by means of an *overdraft*. This form of advance is useful to tide over a period of high expenditure. Suppose, for example, that a retailer wants to borrow up to £5000 in order to build up stocks ready for

Christmas. An arrangement is made with the bank manager for an overdraft limit of £5000. Once this has been done, the retailer can draw cheques to pay suppliers even though there are no funds in the current account. The account becomes 'overdrawn'. The retailer must, however, ensure that this overdraft does not exceed the amount agreed.

The system affords a very convenient way of borrowing:

- the customer does not have to borrow until the money is actually spent;
- as money is received and paid into the bank, the overdraft is automatically reduced;
- there is no fixed schedule of repayments;
- interest is charged only on the amount by which the account is actually overdrawn, and this calculation is made on the daily balance.

An overdraft is often used to finance the sale of goods on credit, since the amount of the overdraft can be reduced as payment for the goods is received.

A second type of advance is called an *ordinary loan*. It provides a lump sum to cover a big expense, such as the purchase of machinery or a car. The bank manager will usually require repayment by regular instalments. A loan of this kind is granted for two or three years at the most, and interest has to be paid whether all the sum is used or not. (Interest on an overdraft is paid only on the actual amount overdrawn). Thus if a borrower knows for how long an advance will be required, a loan may be more convenient; if the exact amount required and the period of borrowing are not known, then an overdraft may be more suitable.

Commercial banks usually prefer to lend for relatively short periods at a time. Overdraft arrangements will be reviewed periodically, usually at least once a year. However, banks may be prepared to lend money long-term for such purposes as house purchase (see page 76).

A bank manager will consider a number of factors before arranging an overdraft or loan for a customer. In the first place, the character of the borrower will be considered. The banker bears great responsibility in granting advances. Any loss due to failure to repay the loan will fall on the bank. The banker must, therefore, make enquiries regarding the personal integrity of the borrower.

Secondly, the banker is entitled to enquire the purpose for

which the advance is required, and will distinguish between a customer seeking funds for speculation and a customer seeking to finance a genuine enterprise. It is not likely that an advance would be granted other than for a legitimate trading purpose.

A further factor to consider is the earning power likely to result from the advance. The banker must take into account that the trader not only has to repay the loan, but has also to pay interest and earn a profit.

In addition to making the enquiries mentioned above, the banker will also ask for some form of *collateral security*. This should be something which the bank can turn into cash should the borrower, for some reason. find it impossible to repay the loan. Some examples of the various kinds of security accepted by a banker are:

- a life assurance policy which has acquired a cash surrender value (this can be assigned to the bank in return for an advance up to the amount of the cash value);
- government stock and shares of public companies (the bank will not usually advance the full market value, since prices fluctuate daily on the stock exchange and allowance must be made for this);
- the title deeds to property (these are regarded as good security although the bank may require the security to be valued by a qualified valuer).

Sometimes a loan to a customer may be secured by a *guarantor*. The guarantor gives a written undertaking to be liable for the customer's debt until it has been paid.

Means of payment

Cheques are a means of transferring the ownership of money. A cheque book contains a set of printed forms and when one of these is properly filled in, it becomes the customer's *instruction* to the bank. There is a counterfoil on which to record the date and the amount of the cheque and to whom it is made payable. Each cheque bears a serial number and other numbers to help the bank in identification and sorting (see Figure 13.2).

The person who writes and signs the cheque is known as the *drawer* of the cheque. The person to whom it is made payable is the *payee* and the bank on which the cheque is drawn is the *drawee*.

Advantages of making payments by cheque

- Cheques save carrying large sums of notes and coins, and so reduce the risk of robbery.
- The bank keeps a record of all payments which helps the drawer and the payee to check their own accounts.
- The passing of a cheque through the bank is accepted as legal evidence of the receipt by the payee of the sum stated on the cheque. Thus the payee is often saved the trouble and expense of sending a receipt.
- Payment may be stopped, if necessary. For example, if a cheque is lost, the bank will stop payment if required to do so.

These advantages are so great that apart from small transactions and sometimes wages, nearly all payments are made through the banks.

On the other hand, a dishonest person may draw a cheque without having the money to back it. Consequently, no-one is obliged to accept a cheque and, in fact, anyone may refuse to do so.

There are two kinds of cheques, namely, *order* and *bearer cheques*. The instruction to the banker on an order cheque reads 'Pay _____ or order'. This is a shortened form of saying 'Pay to _____ or according to their order' and if a cheque is made out in this way, the payee can *endorse* it (by a signature on the back) and hand it to a creditor in payment.

There are three forms of endorsement. An *endorsement in blank* is made when the payee first signs the back of the cheque. The effect of this form of endorsement is to make the cheque payable to 'bearer'. Thus the creditor to whom the payee passes the cheque can either pay it into an account or hand it on to a creditor. A *special endorsement* requires the name of the person to whom or to whose order the cheque is to be made payable. The creditor must also endorse the cheque if using it to settle a debt. Finally, the payee can make a *restrictive endorsement* (by writing on the back of the cheque as shown below) and this prevents the creditor transferring the cheque to anyone else. The cheque must now be paid into an account.

Some cheques are worded 'Pay _____ or bearer' and are payable to anyone who presents the cheque. For this reason bearer cheques are not as safe as order cheques, and are not widely used.

Fig. 13.1   *Cheque endorsements*

S R Thomas	Pay C. Jones S R Thomas	Pay C Jones only S R Thomas
Endorsement in blank	*Special endorsement*	*Restrictive endorsement*

Open and crossed cheques

A *crossed cheque* (Figure 13.1) is so called because it has two parallel lines across it; an *open cheque* does not have them.

The difference between them is that a crossed cheque cannot be cashed across the counter of a bank (the crossing cancels out the order 'to pay on demand'). It must always be paid into a customer's account. An open cheque can be cashed at the branch of the bank it is drawn upon.

Should a crossed cheque fall into some unauthorised person's hands, it could not be cashed. As it must go through an account, the bank is able to trace the presenter of the cheque and therefore the money may not be lost. An open cheque can be cashed over the counter of a bank by an unauthorised person and in this case the money may never recovered. For this reason, it is always safer to use crossed cheques when payments are made.

Fig.13.2   *A crossed cheque*

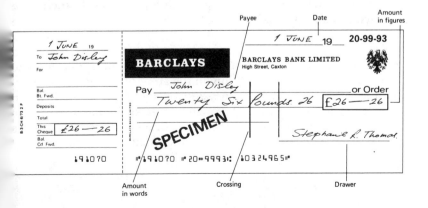

There are two types of crossings:

1 *General crossings* consist of two parallel lines either with or without (*a*) 'and company' or (*b*) 'not negotiable' written between them. Cheques with general crossings can be paid in at any bank for collection.
2 *Special crossings* have a name of a particular bank written between the parallel lines. The cheque can be presented for paying in only at the bank named.

Anyone who takes a cheque in good faith and gives value for it has the right to demand payment, even though it is discovered subsequently that the person who passed it on in payment had stolen it. The drawer of a cheque may be obliged, therefore, to make a double payment: first to the payee, and secondly to the person who had accepted the stolen cheque in good faith from a thief.

In order to avoid this possibility, 'not negotiable' may be written on the cheque. This mean that a person receiving a stolen cheque in all good faith cannot enforce payment.

This type of crossing is not intended to restrict the transferability of a cheque; it acts merely as a warning against accepting such a cheque from a person whose character and integrity are not known.

A further safeguard which can be used is to write 'Account Payee' when making out cheques. The collecting bank will enter the cheque only in the account of the payee, so that a cheque marked in this way cannot be endorsed and passed in payment to someone else.

It will be noted from the above that a cheque is a very safe means of payment. A drawer can direct that a cheque be paid into a particular account (A/c Payee) at a particular branch of a particular bank (special crossing).

Withdrawal of cash
Customers may withdraw cash by writing 'cash' or 'self' after the word 'Pay' on the cheque, filling in the amount on the line below, signing and dating the cheque, and presenting it at the branch where the account is held. To open a crossed cheque in order to draw cash for themselves at their own branch, customers simply write 'pay cash' between the parallel lines and sign beneath (see Figure 13.2).

Fig. 13.3 *Withdrawal of cash*

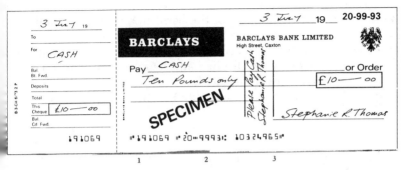

1 The cheque number. Cheque numbers are printed on bank statements to enable customers to identify entries.

2 The bank and branch identifying number. This number enables machines to sort cheques into branch order.

3 The number of the customer's account.

The code line on the cheque illustrates the style of printing adopted by British banks for electronic machine handling of cheques.

A customer wanting to withdraw cash at other branches must make a drawing arrangement beforehand. This is easily done and is useful to people travelling on business or on holiday.

An alternative arrangement is for the customer to obtain a *cheque guarantee card* from the bank. This card carries the name and a specimen signature of the holder, a serial number, the code number of the issuing bank and the date of expiry. By presenting the card at a branch of any of the major British commercial banks, the holder can cash cheques up to a stated limit (at present usually £50).

Stopped cheques

If a drawer has insufficient funds to meet the cheque, the bank refuses to pay it, marks it 'refer to drawer' and returns it to the person who paid it in for collection. Such a cheque is said to be *dishonoured*.

In certain circumstances the bank will also refuse to pay a cheque:

- when the drawer of a cheque requests the bank to stop payment;
- when the bank has received notice of the death of the customer;
- when the bank is notified of the bankruptcy of the customer;
- when the customer closes a current account;
- when the drawer's signature on the cheque differs from the *specimen signature* given to the bank by every new customer at the time the account is opened;
- when a cheque has been altered, and such alteration has not been signed by the drawer;
- when the amount written in words differs from the amount written in figures;
- when the cheque is either *stale* or *post-dated* (see below).

Post-dated cheques   A post-dated cheque is dated for the future. For example, a person who has insufficient funds, at present, to pay a bill may send a cheque which is dated ten days ahead to a creditor. This gives time to find the funds to meet the cheque. Another use of a post-dated cheque it to give the payee time in which to fulfil an obligation (such as , for example, the delivery of goods before a certain date) before it is paid.

Stale cheques   It is usual for cheques to be presented for payment within a few days of being drawn. If, however, a cheque is dated several months earlier than the date it is presented, the bank may require confirmation from the drawer that the cheque is in order before payment is made. Cheques presented six months or so after being drawn are termed 'stale'. They are marked 'out of date' and returned for confirmation to the drawer.

Additional methods of payment

1 Sometimes a personal cheque is not regarded as a satisfactory means of payment. For example, a debtor may not be known personally to a creditor and, because of this, the creditor may refuse to accept a cheque in payment. In such cases it is possible for the debtor to purchase a *draft* from the bank and send this draft to the creditor in settlement of the debt owing. A draft is a cheque drawn on a bank instead of on a person's current account. Thus a draft is acceptable to the creditor because it is guaranteed by the bank itself. There is no risk of it being dishonoured because the person obtaining it has already paid over to the bank the sum for which it was drawn. This form of payment is used in both home and foreign trade.

2 The credit transfer system known as *bank giro* enables both customer and non-customer to pay money conveniently and economically through the banking system. The service may be used for settling individual accounts, or, by issuing one cheque, a customer may be able to have any number of amounts transferred. For example, a number of bills can be paid in this way, or a business may pay salaries to each of its employees using this system. The system may also be used by a bank customer for making deposits whilst away on business or holiday. The transfer is made by completing a form and handing it in to a bank with the cash. The amount is then transferred to the account named on the form.

3 The *standing order* service provides for the automatic payment of regularly recurring, fixed items such as subscriptions, insurance premiums and the like.

4 The *direct debit* system of money transfer differs from the standing order in that it is the supplier who gives payment instructions, and not the buyer. Direct debiting provides for the automatic payment of varying amounts at irregular intervals. Under this arrangement, the supplier sends (*a*) an invoice to the buyer and (*b*) a direct debit form to the buyer's bank. The buyer is saved the trouble of remembering due dates of payment and sending off cheques. Debit transfer can be used also by creditors to claim payments of fixed amounts at regular intervals, as an alternative to standing orders arranged by debtors.

5 Other methods of payment include *budget accounts* and *credit cards* (page 164) and debit cards such as Barclays' Connect.

Additional services

In addition to the three main functions outlined earlier in this chapter, commercial banks offer a number of other services for the convenience of their customers.

1 *Executor* and *trustee* departments will administer customers' wills.

2 *Travellers' cheques* are available to provide a safe way of carrying money when travelling at home or abroad.

3 Arrangements can be made through banks for the purchase or sale of *stocks and shares*.

4 Important documents or small valuables may be placed in *safe custody* at the bank.

5 The *night safe* provides a means of safely depositing notes and coins for customers (such as shopkeepers) who do not end the day's business until after the bank has closed.

6 *Cash dispensers* supply bank notes at any hour of the day and night to customers who hold a cash card supplied by the bank. After inserting the card into the machine, the customer taps out a personal identification number, and the sum required, on the keyboard and the dispenser delivers cash to that amount.

7 Banks will assist with *tax* matters.

8 *Budget* or *planned expenditure accounts* are designed to assist customers with forward budgeting. The customer opens a separate account for the purpose of paying regular bills such as rent, rates, season tickets, gas and electricity. The account is fed by a monthly transfer of a fixed amount from the current account. Thus the budget account will sometimes be overdrawn and sometimes be in surplus. However, as long as cheques drawn on it are for the purposes included in the scheme, the bank will honour them, and the cost of regular items of expenditure can be spread evenly over the year.

9 A bank *credit card*, such as a Barclaycard or an Access card, enables holders to make credit purchases at establishments (shops, hotels, garages, etc.) which have joined the scheme. The advantages to the customer are: (*a*) less cash need be carried; (*b*) a number of bills can be settled with one cheque once a month which could mean a saving on bank charges.

10 An *insurance* service is available to customers. The bank offers advice and obtains commission from insurance companies for policies sold to customers.

11 *References* relating to a customer's financial standing are provided (see page 36).

12 Firms which require cash each week to pay out wages to their employees can make arrangements for it to be available in the form required.

13 *Foreign currency* can be made available.

14 *Information* regarding foreign markets and the financial status of foreign buyers is available to exporters.

Finance for foreign trade

When goods are exported long distances and the foreign buyer requires time before making payments, exporters need to borrow to finance shipments in transit and to provide a period of credit for the foreign importer.

In addition to offering finance in the form of overdrafts and loans, banks will arrange the opening of a *documentary credit*. The foreign importer's bank arranges for a bank in the UK to give the British exporter an irrevocable undertaking to pay in cash for the value of goods as soon as the exporter has presented certain specified documents to them. The documents include a *bill of exchange* (see page 166), the *bill of lading*, (see page 138), and insurance certificates. The exporter receives payment and the bank then claims on the importer's bank abroad, which in turn claims from the importer. After the importer has paid, the bank will release the bill of lading to enable the importer to claim the goods on their arrival.

A variation of the documentary credit system is the *acceptance credit*. This is similar to the method described above, except that on presentation of the documents, the exporter's bank does not provide cash, but irrevocably undertakes to make payment at some time in the future (usually 30, 60, 90, or 180 days later). This irrevocable undertaking of a bank can be sold by the exporter. Thus the latter can get cash at once, but the overseas importer does not have to pay up until the time has elapsed.

Banks may also finance foreign trade by the purchase of *bills of exchange*. Briefly, a bill is a means by which a creditor instructs a debtor to pay a named amount on demand or on a future date. The order may be to pay the creditor or to make payment to someone else. Like a cheque (see page 157), a bill of exchange involves three parties, namely, the *drawer*, the *drawee* and the *payee*. However, whereas a cheque is drawn on a bank, a bill is drawn on a person. Again unlike a cheque, a bill is drawn by the creditor who is very often the drawer and the payee.

In the bill shown in Figure 13.4, H R Thomas is the drawer and the drawee is F Mackenzie. In this example the money is to be paid to the drawer who is, therefore, the payee as well.

After being drawn by H R Thomas the bill is of no value until it has been 'accepted' by F Mackenzie. If the latter is willing to carry out the order, 'accepted' is written across the bill together with a signature. The bill is now described as an 'acceptance' whereas until this stage it was merely a 'draft'.

The importance of the bill of exchange is that it enables the debtor to obtain a period of credit – three months in the following example. Thus goods can be bought and sold before payment is required.

At the same time, the use of a bill of exchange offers advantages to the creditor. An accepted bill is written evidence that the debtor has promised to pay a particular sum on a certain

Fig. 13.4   *A bill of exchange*

BILL OF EXCHANGE   2 December 19—
                                Birmingham
£1000

THREE MONTHS after the date shown pay
to me or my order the sum of One thousand
pounds for value received.

To: F. Mackenzie
     Hong Kong   *H.R. Thomas*

---

date. If the debtor has a sound reputation, then business people
may be prepared to take the accepted bill as payment. Hence, like
cheques, bills can be endorsed and passed on, so that the creditor
may be able to use an accepted bill to settle debts. The person
who holds the bill at the *maturity date* (that is, the date on which
the bill is due for payment) will obtain payment by presenting the
bill to the drawee.

Instead of passing on the bill, a creditor may choose to *discount*
it in order to obtain ready cash. This means that the bill is sold to
a bank for its face value, less interest for the period it has to run.
On the due date the bank will collect the full value of the bill
from the drawee. The discount taken by the bank is known as
banker's discount. It is, in effect, the interest charge made for
money being advanced before the bill matures. The amount of
interest charged will depend on the degree of security of the bill
and the length of time before it becomes due. For example, a
£10 000 bill, bearing a good name and due in three months' time,
might be bought for £9800; whereas if there was doubt concerning ultimate payment, only £9000 might be offered.

A third alternative is for the creditor to hold the bill until
maturity and then ask the bank to collect the sum owing.

If, when the bill is presented on the due date, the debtor does
not pay, the bill is said to be *dishonoured*. When a bank or a
discount house (an institution specialising in the purchase of bills
of exchange) has discounted a bill that is later dishonoured, it will

demand payment from the person who presented the bill for discounting.

Bills of exchange are used mainly in foreign trade. They enable the importer to buy and sell goods before making payment, while at the same time the exporter can obtain cash by discounting the bill with a bank. They also simplify the problems of dealing in different currencies.

13.2 The Bank of England

A central bank is at the heart of the banking system and plays a major part in administering the government's monetary policy. There is normally only one central bank in each country and in Britain it is the Bank of England. The central bank has a number of very special functions.

Functions

Issuing bank notes
The Bank controls the issues of *bank notes*. New notes and coins are put into circulation in return for old ones which are removed by the commercial banks as they deteriorate.

Providing financial services for the government
The Bank acts as banker to the *government*. In the course of this work, it keeps accounts, arranges loans and provides means of payment.

All government revenue (such as proceeds of taxation) is paid to the central bank and payments for goods and services received by the government are made by the Bank. The Bank also keeps the accounts of a number of government departments.

Borrowing by the government is necessary when the revenue received from taxation is insufficient to meet government expenditure. Loans are raised in a number of ways:

- advances made by the Bank to the Treasury are comparable to the overdrafts provided to businesses by the commercial banks;

- long-term loans are obtained by selling new issues of government stock. Registers of stock-holders are kept by the Bank which also pays the interest and arranges transfers and repayments when due.

The accumulated value of annual borrowings by the government is called the *National Debt*; the management of the National Debt is entrusted to the central bank.

In addition to the basic banking functions outlined above, the Bank provides a number of additional services to the government. These include:

- advising on general financial matters such as the level of interest rates or the volume of bank credit (however, the Bank is directly under the control of the *Treasury* and it is the latter which is responsible to Parliament for whatever decisions are taken);
- maintaining relations with international monetary authorities (such as the International Monetary Fund) and with the central banks of other countries.

Overseeing other banks

The Bank has a statutory responsibility to *oversee the activities* of all banks. The core of responsibility is to limit as far as possible the risks to the bank's capital from mis-matched or over-concentrated investment or lending.

Implementing the government's monetary policy

The Bank is responsible for the management of the government's *monetary policy*.

Monetary policy means varying the price and supply of money. The money supply mainly comprises bank deposits, and so monetary controls are intended to regulate this major form of money. Controls are applied by the Bank of England acting on the instructions of the Treasury.

Holding cash reserves

The Bank acts as banker to the commercial banks by holding a proportion of their *cash reserves*. This enables the banks to settle any indebtedness to each other, created by daily clearing of cheques, by transfers between their accounts at the Bank of England. This function is outlined more fully on page 169.

The Bankers' Clearing House

Every day, millions of cheques are being drawn by bank customers and the cheques are subsequently paid into banks by the payees, for the value to be collected on their behalf. A cheque can be paid *only* at the branch on which it is drawn. Therefore, either the payee may take the cheque, if it is not crossed, to that branch for payment in cash, or it must be paid into the payee's bank which in turn must present it for payment at the drawer's bank.

The term *clearing* is used to describe the system of collecting payment for cheques paid into banks; a cheque is said to be cleared when it has been paid by the branch of the bank on which it was drawn.

Fig. 13.5 *The path of a cheque drawn in Birmingham and sent to a payee in Bristol*

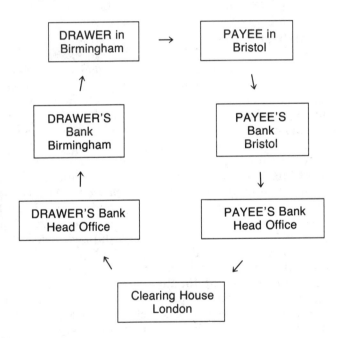

Cheques paid into customers' accounts for collection are sorted out according to the banks on which they are drawn, and listed. At the clearing house, banks exchange cheques drawn on each other. These cheques will be dispatched to the branches on which they are drawn.

At the end of each day, each bank compiles a statement which shows, on the left-hand side, sums owing from other banks (these amounts will be in payment for cheques delivered to other banks); on the right-hand side entries are made for sums owing to the other banks (for cheques delivered by them). The two sides are totalled and a balance worked out for the net sum due to be received or paid by the bank in respect of all its transactions for that day.

Each bank keeps an account at the Bank of England and it is to and from that account that the balance for the day's clearing operations is transferred.

The main clearing house is in London and the time taken to clear a cheque is about three to four days.

In addition to cheques, the Bankers' Clearing House deals also with the interchange of *standing orders* between the banks. It also processes data relating to *bank giro credits*, and debits originating under the *direct debiting* scheme, on behalf of customers of the banks.

13.3   Merchant Banks

The merchant banks are found almost exclusively in London. They are specialised banks which help *industry* and *commerce* in particular ways. The original merchant bankers were prosperous merchants who began to perform various financial services for small traders; gradually the financial side of the business grew more important until eventually they gave up trade and concentrated on banking.

One of the main functions of the merchant banks is the provision of *credit* for financing *foreign trade*. An acceptance credit is arranged by an importer in London with one of the merchant banks. The credit is opened in favour of the exporter abroad who, when the goods have been shipped, draws a bill of exchange for the amount due.

The bill is an order addressed by the seller to the buyer, or to the merchant bank acting for the seller, to pay a certain sum of money on a certain date – usually three months distant. This bill is sent to London where it is 'accepted' by the bank. The bill then becomes a document which can be sold or discounted. The cash, less discount, can be secured immediately by the seller.

The accepted bill of exchange commands this ready market largely on the strength of the name of the merchant bank. When the bill comes to maturity the accepting bank has to pay over the amount stated on the bill to whoever presents it and will expect to receive the necessary funds from the exporter who drew the bill, a few days before maturity.

A second function of the merchant banks is to act as *issuing houses* for companies making issues of *shares* or *loan stocks* (see page 93). An issuing house will advise on the type of security to be offered, the method and time of issue, and the terms of the offer. It will also negotiate with the Council of the Stock Exchange for a quotation and assist in the preparation of the prospectus.

In addition to arranging issues, the merchant banks also *underwrite* them (i.e. in return for a commission, they undertake to buy any shares which cannot be sold to the public), and arrange for payment of dividends as they fall due.

Merchants banks also engage in the following activities:

- management of investments for pension funds, charities and unit trusts;
- dealing in foreign exchange;
- financing mergers and take-overs;
- provision of specialist advice in arranging loans to industry.

Many merchant banks also perform the more usual banking facilities such as servicing current accounts, but only on a limited scale.

13.4 Savings Banks

As their name suggests, savings banks were originally formed with the aim of encouraging saving, especially by people with small incomes.

The *Trustee Savings Bank* is now a public limited company and has developed from a small savings bank into a major institution offering banking facilities similar to those offered by commercial banks.

The *National Savings Bank* operates under the control of the government's Department of National Savings. It operates through the network of post offices. There are two types of account: the ordinary and the investment account. Both interest and capital are guaranteed by the government and money deposited is invested in government securities.

The savings banks have played an important part in the *National Savings Movement* through which millions of small savers have lent money to the government in times both of war and of peace.

13.5   Girobank

Girobank offers banking facilities through the post office network. A Giro service is one in which all accounts are held at a single computer centre. Instead, therefore, of using cheques which pass from drawer to payee (who probably have accounts at different banks), payments between account holders can be made by sending transfer instructions to the centre. Drawer and payee are informed by the Girobank Centre that the transfer has been made.

Girobank now provides most of the services available through the commercial banks (see Section 13.1). For example, deposit and current accounts are available as well as standing orders, direct debit transfers, travellers' cheques, foreign currency, budget accounts, credit transfers (*Transcash*), loans, overdrafts and cheque guarantee cards. It enjoys an advantage over the commercial banks in that post offices are open for longer hours.

13.6   Post Office Money Transfer Services

Stamps
Postage stamps are sometimes used to settle small payments by post. The receiver can either use them for sending post or sell them back to the Post Office.

Postal orders
Orders are issued for varying amounts. In addition to the amount of the order, poundage is charged to cover the cost to the Post Office of handling this form of payment. A counterfoil is attached to the order and should be completed and retained by the sender in case the postal order is lost and a claim is made on the Post Office.

Like cheques, postal orders may be *crossed* so that payment will only be made into a bank account.

Registered post
Bank notes can be posted in a registered envelope and insured against loss. A special registration fee is payable and when the envelope is posted a receipt is obtained from the Post Office.

Cash on delivery (COD)
This service is useful to firms wanting payment on delivery of the goods. The buyer pays the postman/woman when delivery is made. Mail-order firms often use this service.

13.7 Building Societies

Traditionally the purpose of a building society was to obtain funds from members and to make loans for the purchase of houses. In recent years, the societies have developed a wide range of other services such as the provision of standing orders, current accounts, credit cards and cash dispensers. The Building Societies Act, which came into force on 1 January 1987, greatly extends the range of banking services that societies may provide. The new services include the following:

- personal loans;
- money transmission services (including standing orders and direct debits);
- foreign exchange facilities;
- insurance facilities.

From 1988, building societies can change their legal status to public companies.

Test Yourself

1 Write down the main functions of the commercial banks.
2 An account upon which interest is paid is called _____; an account on which cheques may be drawn is called _____.
3 Which document shows a customer the balance on his or her current account?
4 Advances offered by a commercial bank may take a number of forms. What are they?
5 Give an example of the use of an overdraft.
6 List the factors which a bank manager must consider before arranging an advance.
7 Give examples of collateral security.
8 Briefly describe how commercial banks provide finance for exports.
9 Write down the names of two kinds of cheque.
10 Write down the names of two types of crossing.
11 Write down an example of (*a*) an endorsement in blank and (*b*) a restrictive endorsement.
12 How can a cheque be made payable into a particular bank account?
13 What is a cheque guarantee card?
14 Write down three advantages of using cheques as means of payment.

15 What is a dishonoured cheque?
16 Write down eight examples of situations in which a bank will refuse to pay a cheque.
17 Give an example of the use of a post-dated cheque.
18 How does a bank draft differ from a cheque?
19 Describe briefly how bank giro is useful to (*a*) a person without a current account and (*b*) a business firm.
20 Name four other methods of payment through a bank for settlement of transactions.
21 List the various services available to customers of a commercial bank.
22 Name five functions of the Bank of England.
23 What is the National Debt?
24 What is monetary policy?
25 Write down two functions of merchant banks.
26 How does payment through Girobank differ from payment through a bank?
27 Write down the various Post Office money transfer services.
28 State the new legal status available to building societies from 1988.

Chapter 14

Transport

Transport is one of the *aids to trade*. It brings supplies of raw materials to factories and delivers finished goods to wholesalers and retailers (see Chapter 1).

Improvements in transport have raised the standard of living.

- Consumers are provided with an increasing variety of goods (including foods) from all over the world.
- By drawing supplies from, and selling goods to, all parts of the world, large factories can produce on a big scale. Generally, the greater the quantity of goods that can be produced, the cheaper they can be sold to consumers.
- The movement of raw materials and fuel over long distances enables regions and countries to specialise in producing commodities. Specialisation results in certain benefits, chiefly more and cheaper goods (see Chapter 1). Any surplus can be exchanged for commodities produced by other countries.

The cost of transport is a significant influence on industrial location. A major decision which business people have to take concerns the geographical location of firms; obviously, their aim will be to locate an enterprise where the costs of production are lowest. One of the major costs of production is that of transport – the transport of raw materials to a factory and the transport of finished products to consumers. The costs of transporting raw materials can be reduced by locating a factory as near to their source as possible; alternatively, the costs of distribution can be reduced by locating a factory as near to the market as possible. There are, therefore, two possible courses of action to follow, and the actual course adopted will depend very largely on the nature of the industry.

A trader has the choice of many different forms of transport by land, sea or air. Each form has its own particular advantages and disadvantages and the trader must choose. In this chapter, the various forms of transport will be considered, together with their advantages and disadvantages.

14.1   Road Transport

A trader who has a consignment of goods ready for dispatch may choose between a number of different methods of sending it by road.

National carriers
If the goods have to be sent to a distant destination they can be carried in vehicles owned by general carriers.

Local carriers
For a shorter distance, the trader may hire a local carrier. In most areas there are small transport businesses owned by people who earn a living by carrying goods for traders.

Trader's own vehicle
Very often a trader owns a van which is used to deliver goods to customers.

Advantages of road transport

- *Flexibility*   Motor vehicles can go anywhere where a road exists. Transport by railway or canal is limited to places on the line of the route, whereas motor vehicles can go into the warehouse or factory for loading the goods and take them straight to the unloading point. When goods are sent by rail they have to be collected by road from the sender, unloaded at the goods station and reloaded on to railway trucks. The process is reversed when goods arrive at their destination. The railways have overcome this problem to some extent by the use of 'containers' which can be carried by road vehicles or by train. Containers obviate the necessity for unloading and reloading goods at stations.
- *Cheapness*   A road haulier requires little capital compared with railways which have to construct their own permanent way. The roads are provided for all road users and all that is required by a road haulier is the capital cost of a vehicle and payment of its running costs. Consequently road transport charges are generally lower than railway freight rates.

- *Speed* Roads are faster than railways and aircraft for short journeys. By the time goods are taken to the station or airport, loaded, transported, unloaded and taken to their destination, the journey could have been made in less time by transporting directly in a road vehicle.

When a trader's *own vehicle* is used to deliver goods to customers there are certain advantages in addition to those listed above. In the first place, the goods are under the trader's control until the actual delivery to the buyer, so that the risk of theft and damage from careless handling is reduced. Secondly, goods can be sent out whenever the trader wishes. There are no delays as might occur if delivery was dependent upon trains or road carriers. Thirdly, the vehicle may be used to bring back empty containers (if these are used in the business); and finally, the vehicle can advertise the trader's business.

On the other hand, these benefits must be weighed against a number of drawbacks. The capital cost of buying a vehicle may be relatively heavy and the running costs must also be considered. There are certain *fixed costs* which have to be paid whether the vehicle is used regularly or infrequently. If the vehicle cannot be fully employed, the cost of using it per mile may be higher than the charges of independent carriers. For example, a return load is necessary if the cost per mile is to be minimised, and the use of the vehicle become uneconomical if it has to return empty. These factors have caused many large businesses to hand over their distribution to transport specialists. In many instances, they have sold their own fleet to a transport company which continues to run the vehicles under the original name. In addition, large businesses may prefer to contract out when increasingly specialised techniques of efficient delivery can be better handled by a transport firm. For example, the transport of flowers, plants and foodstuffs demands purpose-built vehicles and a temperature-controlled environment.

14.2 Rail Transport

Advantages of rail transport

- Railways have the advantage over motor vehicles for the transport of large quantities of heavy, bulky goods such as coal. A train crew can convey a considerable tonnage in one train load whereas a large number of lorries and drivers are needed to move the same quantity by road.

- Railways are faster than road transport over long journeys. Road transport is handicapped by traffic congestion in towns not yet bypassed by motorways, and heavy lorries are slow on long distances. The opening of the Channel tunnel will mean that many of the times now achievable by air freight to Europe will be equalled by the tunnel train service.

The *freightliner* service is the fastest way of carrying goods over medium and long distances. The freightliner network is based on the *container* as the unit of load (see page 184). Containers can be moved from road to rail and possibly back to road again, or direct to the holds of ships. Express freight trains operate at high speed and the transfer of containers at freightliner terminals between road and rail can be accomplished very quickly.

At present, few British routes are long enough to give container trains an 'edge' over road transport. This is likely to change dramatically when the Channel tunnel is opened in 1993 and the amount of international freight carried by British Rail is expected to more than treble. Much of it is likely to be in container loads. In addition to speed, the freightliner service has further significant advantages.

- *Reliability*   Express freight trains run to a timetable which means that firms can plan their deliveries with certainty.
- *Safety*   The containers are packed with goods at the manufacturer's depot. Hence the possibility of pilfering and damage when loose parcels are handled during unloading and reloading at stations is eliminated.
- *Large capacity*   The movement of large capacity containers by train means that no job is too extensive to tackle.
- *Reserved space*   Train-space may be reserved in advance, which means the elimination of delays at the freightliner terminal.

Parcels for delivery within Britain and to many European countries can be sent by *passenger train*. Items which must reach their destination before a certain time, such as newspapers and mail, are often sent by scheduled passenger trains.

Freight rates

1 Rail freight charges become cheaper with distance: the charge per mile falls as the distance increases.

2 Charges decrease with weight: thus heavy bulk goods such as coal can be carried relatively cheaply.

14.3   Sea Transport

Sea transport can be considered under two categories:

- ocean shipping;
- coastal shipping.

Ocean shipping

Ocean shipping transports goods across the seas of the world.

Although there are many different kinds of ships, they can be conveniently divided into two main groups; *tramp* vessels and *cargo liners*.

Tramps

Tramp vessels are ships that go wherever they can obtain cargo. They have no set routes nor do they sail at fixed times. In a way they are like taxis that ply for hire; they will pick up cargo at any port and carry it to any destination in the world. The cargo carried is usually bulk consignments of commodities such as coal, ores, wheat, timber, rice and liquids.

It is essential for the owners of tramp vessels to get in touch with shippers of bulk cargoes all over the world. This is done through a market called a *Shipping Exchange*, such as the Baltic Exchange in London. The Baltic Exchange is the world's largest market for the chartering of ships of all nationalities.

The owner of a tramp vessel seeking work for the ship informs a *shipping broker* who is a member of the Exchange. On the floor of the Exchange the broker meets other brokers who represent prospective charterers of ships. The charterers are the importers and exporters of bulk cargoes. Charterers inform their brokers of their requirements, and indicate the type of ship wanted, the dates of loading and destination. The brokers bargain over the rates to be charged for the transport of the cargo. Tramp freight rates depend upon demand for, or the supply of, shipping and may fluctuate.

The contract between the owners and the charterers is known as the *charter party*. A *voyage charter* hires the ship for a particular voyage or number of voyages, whilst a *time charter* hires it for a certain period of time regardless of the number of voyages.

Thus the Baltic Exchange is a centre where information concerning the availability of shipping space and the type and quantities of cargo for shipment to various ports is brought together. Freight rates are determined by the brokers representing ship-owners and cargo-owners from all over the world.

Cargo liners
Unlike tramps, liners work to fixed schedules and timetables. Liner companies have offices and agents in important commercial centres and usually make their own arrangments for obtaining cargo (which is generally made up of numerous consignments sent by different exporters). In addition to cargo, liners usually carry passengers. They are also used to carry mail.

Liner owners organise *conferences* for fixing rate for carrying cargo. They provide shippers of goods with a regular service: like trains, liners journey regularly on set routes, whether full or empty.

Coastal shipping

A large volume of goods is carried between the chief ports of the UK by tramps and liners on regular coastal routes. Coal, cement and iron ore form the bulk of the material carried.

14.4   Inland Waterways

Inland waterways comprise navigable rivers (such as the Thames, Severn, Mersey and Tyne) and canals. In Britain, canals were built in the 18th century to transport bulky raw materials. They declined as a result of the development of rail transport and by the mid-20th century, had largely fallen into disuse. However, efforts have been made in recent years to increase the use of waterways. For example, barge-carrying ship systems, such as BACAT, have been developed to link the interior of the UK with the inland waterways of Europe: barges are taken aboard a 'mother ship' for the sea crossing and then continue their journey inland by canal.

Advantages of inland waterways

- Water transport is cheaper than land transport because of the low energy cost. An engine of a given capacity can haul a greater load on water than it can on land, The low cost of carriage makes water transport particularly suitable for the movement of heavy, relatively cheap goods such as coal, clay and lime.
- Carriage by barge or narrowboat provides a smooth ride and this method of transport is suitable for articles such as pottery, which are easily broken.

Disadvantages of inland waterways

- Most inland waterways are so narrow that the speed of boats is severely restricted, in case the wash damages the banks. The need to pass through frequent locks in hilly country causes further delay.
- In winter the waterway may freeze and stop transport completely for a time.
- Inland waterways can only deliver goods directly to places situated on the sides of rivers or canals. Delivery to firms situated elsewhere requires the use of road or rail transport to complete the journey, with the consequent possibility of loss from increased handling required.
- Waterways and locks vary so much in size that only a narrow boat can travel throughout the waterways system. Widening of waterways is restricted because at points in their courses many are bordered by valuable business properties.

14.5 Air Transport

Traders can *charter* aircraft as they do tramp ships. The principal air charter market is at the Baltic Exchange where freight rates are arranged between the brokers. Freight rates are based on weight and are not affected by the value of the goods.

Advantages of air transport

- The principal advantage of air transport is speed. For example, a flight from London to Frankfurt in West Germany takes about three hours; the same journey by road takes 15 hours.

- Aircraft can travel long distances over land and sea without unloading and reloading freight.
- A smooth passage means that danger of damage to delicate articles is reduced. In addition the relatively quick journey time means that shorter periods of insurance cover are required than for sea transport. Consequently insurance rates may be lower than those charged for sea transport.

Disadvantages of air transport

- Bad weather may restrict flights.
- Costly airports are required at either end of the journey and these sites have to be built on the outskirts of towns because modern aircraft require very long runways.Thus goods may have to be taken a considerable distance by road or rail before and after the flight. For journeys between towns within a country more time may be spent in travelling between the airports and the town centres than is taken by actual air journey. However, for long flights abroad time lost in travelling to and from the airports is negligible when put against the time saved in flight,
- Air is more costly than land and sea transport. A very substantial drop in rates will be necessary before air freight rates become directly competitive with those of surface-borne cargo.

Uses of air transport

Air transport is suitable for the carriage of high-value, low-bulk goods such as chemicals and jewellery. Mail is also carried and air courier firms deliver important documents and parcels abroad.

A new development is carrying parts for machines and even raw materials for industry. This is part of 'just-in-time' stock control achieved through the use of computers. If a business can rely on an express courier service for bringing in raw materials, the expense of the air freight can be offset by savings on the cost of holding stock.

Competition with shipping

Although the size of load an aircraft can carry by comparison with a ship is small, goods sent by air do not require packing in heavy and costly crates and the lighter packing may save customs duties when these are levied on weight. Thus when delivery is urgent, air freighting may offer a favourable alternative to sea transport.

Hovercraft

The hovercraft is a vehicle which rides on a cushion of air over both *land and water*. Regular hovercraft coastal services operate in certain areas of British waters and there is a cross-Channel service to France.

Hovercraft are a useful form of transport for short-range ferry routes and general purpose transport over difficult terrain.

14.6 Pipelines

Pipelines are used for transporting commodities such as liquids (e.g. oil and petrol), gases (e.g. natural gas) and, of course, water. This form of transport may be used to transfer commodities long distances over land and under the sea. It has developed in recent years for a number of reasons. Rising fuel costs make pipelines an attractive economic alternative to other forms of transport in certain circumstances. Once installed either underground or under the sea, pipelines cause less damage to the environment than alternative methods of transport. Safety in transferring flammable commodities is another important consideration. In addition, maintenance costs are relatively low.

On the other hand, pipelines are costly to install and installation in built-up areas may prove difficult. Furthermore, the range of commodities which can be transported in this way is limited and generally a pipeline is usable only for a single type of product.

14.7 Ports and Docks

Ports are of great importance to trade because they facilitate the loading and discharging of goods of all kinds. The control of a port lies with the *port authority* and the work of this body can be divided into two main categories: activities dealing with ships and work dealing with cargo.

Ships

In order to make navigation safe for shipping, the port authority keeps a channel clear by dredgers, and marks it with buoys and lights. When a vessel comes near a port, it is usually boarded by a pilot who advises the ship's master. Traffic rules are also drawn up and deal with such matters as signals, lights and prohibited anchorages. Towage services are provided by both the port authority and private firms, who operate tugs to help large vessels in and out of the docks.

All large ports carry out maintenance work and ship repairs, often in dry docks, which allow engineers and painters to work on the underwater parts of a vessel's hull.

All ports provide ships with supplies of fresh water as well as fuel.

Cargo

In order to facilitate the handling and storing of cargo, a dock authority provides equipment in the form of quays, cranes, hoists, transit sheds (to provide cover for goods being loaded or unloaded) and warehouses specially equipped to store such commodities as frozen meat, dairy produce, leaf tobacco, and wool.

The movement of cargo requires the use of road vehicles and rail trucks. Thus the layout of the port will include loading bays for all forms of land transport. In addition, if the port is used by passengers, landing stages and baggage halls for customs examination will be provided.

The port authority will carry out for an importer all the work of landing, weighing and transporting cargo to a warehouse. The details of the goods received from the ship, as well as particulars such as when warehousing rent begins, are entered on a *landing account*. Any damage discovered on landing is noted on the landing account, otherwise the port authority is responsible for damage subsequently found.

Containerisation

The introduction of the container has been a very important development in international freight transport. The theory behind containerisation is that by packing goods into a large metal container at the consignor's depot and transporting it by the most convenient method directly to its destination, handling time and cost of transport are considerably reduced. These advantages are applicable to the movement of goods by road, rail and air, but it is in the shipping industry that containers have made the most obvious changes.

The conventional method of handling ships' cargo was to load a quantity of items on wooden *palettes* and transfer the palettes by crane in or out of the ship's hold. Much time and labour was involved in loading and unloading the palettes, as well as in checking and storing an assortment of cases, crates, cartons and bales.

Nowadays modern berths are purpose-built for standard sized containers, and heavy, containerised cargo is loaded and unloaded by cranes. Lighter kinds of 'bulk cargo' such as loose grain or seeds, are discharged by suction elevators working on the principle of a vacuum cleaner.

The use of containers cuts the handling charge at ports. The faster turn-round and the generally higher operating speed of modern container ships enables each one to carry, on average, as much cargo during a year as six to ten conventional ships.

Whilst containerisation results in considerable benefits, it does require a large investment of capital in the containers themselves and in handling equipment.

14.8 Factors Influencing The Choice of Transport

The trader has a choice of different forms of transport for goods. How is a choice to be made? The main considerations are outlined below.

1 The nature of the commodity to be transported is an important factor. It may be bulky, valuable, perishable or fragile, and the type of transport used must be selected with the nature of the commodity in mind.
2 The purpose of the journey must also be considered, that is, whether goods are needed urgently or not.
3 The geographical situations of the sender and the consignee are important. It is probable that not all forms of transport will be available for the journey to be undertaken. For instance, in the UK a great many more places can be reached by road than by air, water or rail. Sometimes a combination of means of transport will have to be used, particularly when goods are exported abroad.
4 The quantity of the commodity to be transported is an important consideration. Rail freight charges, for example, decrease with weight.

5 Another factor is the actual cost of the transport. For example, an article with a low selling price will have a small profit margin so that transport must not add substantially to costs.

Test Yourself

1 How does transport aid trade?
2 How does transport raise the standard of living?
3 State briefly how the cost of transport influences industrial location.
4 Name three types of road transport.
5 Write down three advantages of road transport.
6 What are (*a*) the benefits and (*b*) the drawbacks of the use of a trader's own vehicle?
7 Roads are faster than rail and air transport for _____ journeys.
8 Rail transport is faster than road transport for _____ journeys.
9 Write down four advantages of freightliners.
10 Which ships (*a*) work to fixed schedules and timetables, (*b*) go wherever cargo can be found?
11 Where is the shipping freight market located in the UK?
12 What is a Charter Party?
13 What is (*a*) a Time Charter and (*b*) a Voyage Charter?
14 How are shipping freight rates determined?
15 Why have canals declined as a means of transport?
16 List two advantages of air transport.
17 List two disadvantages of air transport.
18 What is a hovercraft?
19 Briefly describe how pipelines form a method of transport.
20 What is containerisation?
21 What is a landing account?

Chapter 15

Communications

Communication means the sending of information from one person or firm to another. Information may be transmitted in the following forms:

- written e.g. letters, postcards and telemessages;
- spoken e.g. telephone and radio.

Increasingly, businesses are using computer-based systems for communications. Integrated computer systems capable of handling text, data, voice and images are available to provide the business user with a complete information-processing facility. Work stations situated at different locations can be linked to the computer network to provide distributed data-processing facilities.

In this chapter, the different methods of communications are described and examined in relation to commerce.

15.1 Methods of Communication

Written communications

The urgency of the message is the factor which decides how it is sent. Those messages that are less urgent are sent through the post.

Letters and postcards
These form the major means of written communication used in the business world. Postcards are used only for messages which are short (such as orders for goods or acknowledgements of receipts) and not of a private nature.

Inland letters may be sent in the following ways.

187

Ordinary post   There are two classes of service known as first and second class. The latter is cheaper and mail is usually delivered up to one working day later than first class. The charges for both classes depend upon the weight and size of letters or cards.

In order to handle a growing volume of letters and cards, the Royal Mail uses high-speed machine sorting. The efficient use of machines requires the use of (*a*) letter envelopes and cards of standardised shapes and sizes known as *Post Office Preferred*; and (*b*) postcodes. A *postcode* is a group of letters and figures which represents an address in abbreviated form. The first part represents the postal delivery district of the town and the second the street, part of street or even building where the letter has to be delivered.

A typical postcoded address is:

> Mr R Nicholls
> 76 Honor Avenue
> WOLVERHAMPTON
> WV4 5HH

Business reply   This facility is available for firms to use under licence to encourage a reply from clients by not putting them to the expense of paying postage. The users of this service enclose in their communications an unstamped reply card, letter card, envelope, folder or gummed label of a special design. The addressee pays the postal charges on all the replies received. The system is of particular use to advertisers as a means of encouraging replies from prospective customers.

Freepost   This is another form of business reply service. However, instead of the user enclosing a form of reply in the communication, a special address is included. Replies bearing this address can be posted in the ordinary way but without a stamp. Postage is paid by the addressee on all replies received.

Freepost offers some advantage over the business reply service in that the advertiser saves stationery costs.

Express   Express services for speedy delivery are available in a variety of forms, such as, for example, the conveyance of a postal packet all the way by Royal Mail messenger at the sender's request. Various *private postal services* are also available for handling high-speed letters and documents. They include: delivery around London and other large cities by motorcycle or van; guaranteed overnight delivery services throughout Britain; and 24-hour international deliveries.

Registration   Any first class letter may be registered or insured against loss. Thus registered letter post is useful for sending money or articles of value such as jewellery. The benefits of this service include: special security handling; proof of posting; signature on delivery; and various levels of compensation. *Consequential loss insurance* (see page 198) is available for sending items which could be worth more than their material value.

Recorded delivery   This service provides a record of the posting and delivery of a postal packet and limited compensation in the event of loss or damage in the post. This service is specially suitable for sending documents and papers of little or no monetary value.

Certificate of posting   If proof of posting an unregistered letter is required, a certificate of posting may be obtained from the post office free of charge.

Poste restante   This service permits letters and parcels to be addressed to any post office (except a town sub-office) for subsequent collection by the addressee. Poste restante is a service provided solely for the convenience of travellers (such as sales representatives) and it may not be used in the same town for more than three months.

Private boxes   A private box may be rented at a delivery office for the reception of letters and parcels to be called for. This service provides an alternative to delivery by the Royal Mail at the place of address and it enables business firms to pick up corres-pondence at the most convenient times. The service is also a useful safeguard against the misdelivery of letters. In addition, it enables the addressee to conceal his or her name if so desired, and in this case correspondence is addressed to a box number. An annual fee is payable to the Post Office for the use of a private box number.

Private bags   Individual lockable bags may be rented for the purpose of taking mail to and from the post office. This service offers a form of security and ease of handling.

Selectapost   The Royal Mail will, upon request, sort a firm's incoming mail into departments before delivery. Hence, it is possible for a firm to save the employees' time which would be taken up with this routine task.

Mailsort   Large business firms which pre-sort their mail are offered a saving on their postage bills.

Datapost   Documents and other items may be sent by this courier service which offers speedy and reliable delivery. Overnight or same-day deliveries are available. If delivery is not on time as guaranteed, payment is refunded.

Electronic post   This Royal Mail service is useful to a firm which wants to send a large quantity of standard letters to different addresses. The letters and envelopes required can be produced at an Electronic Post Centre using computer and laser printing technology, prior to delivery. The service is useful, for example, as a means of circulating customers or company shareholders.

International postal service   The Universal Postal Union, to which most countries belong, controls the international letter post. Letters and postcards for Europe are sent by air, but communications to other countries may be sent either by surface mail or air mail. The latter is quicker but more expensive.

Telemessages and overseas telegrams
A telephone message of up to 50 words may be sent for delivery by the postman/woman on the next working day.
   Overseas telegrams (sometimes termed 'cables') may be sent to most parts of the world, to ships in port, to aircraft at airports and to trains at railway stations abroad.

Telex
The telex service enables written messages to be teleprinted at the receiver's end.
   Business firms may rent a telex installation from British Telecom. The United Kingdom telex service is fully automatic and immediate connection is made by direct dialling to any subscriber. Similarly many subscribers abroad may be obtained by direct dialling.

   Telex and telemessages are examples of data transmission services. Other examples include teletex, electronic mail and facsimile transmission (fax).

Teletex
Teletex is a fully automatic international service for sending messages between terminals (such as, for example, computers or electronic typewriters with a teletex adapter). Messages can be

sent more speedily than by telex. They are sent memory to memory, which means that messages can be prepared, stored and sent when appropriate.

Electronic mail
Printed messages are sent and received using computers linked to a telephone system by means of a modem. The latter is a device which enables computer users to send and receive data over telephone lines. *Telecom Gold* is an electronic mail service which allows printed messages to be sent at high speed to an electronic mailbox, or to a number of different mailboxes simultaneously.

Facsimile systems (fax)
Drawings, photographs, typed or printed information, documents, etc., may be reproduced and transmitted to many places in the world via the telephone network. Public facsimile services include the Royal Mail's *Intelpost* and British Telecom's *Bureaufax*.

Videotex
This is a term used to describe any computer-based system which allows text to be received and displayed on a screen. Transmission of text by a television signal is called *teletext*. Examples include the BBC and ITV information services called *Ceefax* and *Oracle*. Where telephone lines are used for transmission, the term *viewdata* is applied. *Prestel* is a registered trade mark for British Telecom's public viewdata service. It can be used by business, public libraries and private individuals. A user can have either a Prestel set or a computer linked to the telephone line with a modem. The service provides access to many thousands of pages of specialist information. Unlike teletext services (where information is only received), Prestel is a two-way system because users can receive information and send messages to other users or to the information providers. For example, a *Prestel* user can order goods, book a hotel or buy services such as insurance.

Individual businesses can have private viewdata systems for use within their organisations.

Spoken communications

Telephone
The telephone enables business people to contact each other

over any distance. The major advantage over written communications is that one conversation can cover the ground of both question and answer, with the additional advantage that in conversation a business person's views can be adapted quickly in the light of those of the other person. Thus hours of letter-writing can often be avoided by a single phone call.

The *Freephone* service enables calls to be made to a number via the operator without cost to the caller. The service is useful to business firms for encouraging customers. The *Linkline* service is similar except that calls may be made direct. Customers may call Linkline 0800 free or Linkline 0345 at a local charge for long distance calls.

Radiophones
These phones are useful for business people who travel and need to keep in touch with business colleagues or with customers. Models can be carried in a briefcase or installed in a car. Mobile radiopayphones are also available on certain mainline rail routes, on selected ferry routes and on certain express coaches. Mobile radiophones use the cellular radio networks, which are being extended by Cellnet and Vodafone (the only two companies licensed to operate cellular radio) to most of the United Kingdom. The cellular system is based on radio transmitters, which pick calls up and pass them to exchanges linked to the public network. A cell is the geographic area that a transmitter covers.

Radiopaging
Radiopaging is another form of staff locating system and is available nationwide. Originally, it was a 'bleeper' signal system which required the receiver to telephone the sender. The latest radiopagers can receive and display written messages thus avoiding the need for staff to make telephone contact.

Voicemail
This voice message facility allows a telephone caller to send messages when a business is closed. The messages are stored and retrieved later by telephone at the convenience of the recipient.

Phonecards
These are useful as a form of cashless calling. The small, green plastic cards allow payment for calls in advance and can be bought at post offices and at retail outlets which display the Phonecard logo. Credit calls can also be made using credit cards such as Visa and Access. Calls are charged to the customer's credit card.

Overseas telephone calls can, in many cases, be dialled direct, or, if not, may be made via the operator.

Directories　　British Telecom publishes various types of telephone directories. The main types are:

- alphabetical directories;
- classified business directories e.g. Yellow Pages, Europages.

These directories are distributed free to all subscribers in the areas in which they reside. In addition, British Telecom will supply on request directories of any town or district in any country to which a telephone service is available.

There are also competing private directories such as *Thomson's Local Directory*.

Radio
Radio is used as a method of communication by the police, the fire service, taxicab companies and many others. Radio stations broadcast regular weather bulletins to aid ships at sea, and road reports to assist drivers to avoid areas of heavy traffic congestion.

Confravision
British Telecom has opened television studios in various major cities, which can be used for business conferences. Groups of people in different cities are able to conduct meetings as though they were all in the same room. This service permits face-to-face 'meetings' between business people without the inconvenience of long-distance travel. *Videostream* is a similar sound and vision service available in the UK and internationally. Special studios are not required. An *audio-conferencing* service permits groups of people at various locations to conduct a business meeting, using the telephone as a link.

15.2　The Work of the Post Office and British Telecom

The Post Office is a public corporation which performs banking functions (see Chapter 13) and provides inland and overseas postal services. British Telecom is a separate public limited company and provides inland and overseas telecommunications such as telex and telephone systems.

Neither the Post Office nor British Telecom has a monopoly in these methods of communication. Private operators are permitted to carry urgent or valuable mail; and other telephone networks, such as Mercury, link major business centres.

The *Post Office Guide* is the official handbook of the Post Office and is published periodically. The Guide gives full particulars of the principal services and charges. The *British Telecom Guide* provides information on telecommunications services and charges.

15.3 The Importance of Communications

Modern, speedy methods of transporting goods have made the world into a single market. Side by side with the speeding-up of transport has gone as great a speeding-up of methods for sending information.

Modern means of communication assist commerce in the following ways.

- Information concerning the state of a market – whether there is an abundance or shortage of a commodity – enables those engaged in commerce to move goods more efficiently to where they are required.
- Telephone and data transmission services enable traders to make immediate contact even though they live hundreds or thousands of miles apart.
- The postal system provides a means for the transfer of documents used during a business transaction (see Chapter 4).

Test Yourself

1 What is the meaning of 'communication' in commerce?
2 Communication may be written or _____.
3 What is the meaning of Post Office Preferred?
4 Why has a postal coding system been established?
5 How does the business reply service differ from Freepost?
6 List the differences between registration and recorded delivery.
7 What is a certificate of posting?
8 What is the purpose of poste restante?
9 What is the advantage of renting a private box?
10 List the advantages of telex.
11 State four other examples of data transmission services.

12 Write down the two main types of telephone directories provided by the Post Office.
13 Briefly describe the use of radio as a form of communication.
14 What is 'confravision'?
15 Which publication provides particulars of the services provided by the Post Office?
16 Briefly describe how communications assist commerce.

Chapter 16

Insurance

There are a number of services involved in bringing goods from producer to consumer, and insurance is one of these services or *aids to trade*. In buying and selling goods a number of risks must be taken which, if they occur, involve traders in financial losses. For example, premises may be damaged or destroyed by fire; goods may be stolen; employees may be injured in the course of their work. These hazards, and many others, may be *insured* against. In return for a payment known as a *premium*, an *insurance company* will agree to compensate the insured person in the event of a particular loss or group of losses during the period of insurance.

16.1 The Principle of Insurance

Insurance is based upon the principle of the fortunate helping the unfortunate. Records show that, every year a certain number of business premises are destroyed by fire, so many accidents occur, etc. What is not known is which particular property or persons will be affected. But if a large number of people, liable to the same risk, are willing to join together, a common fund can be set up from which compensation can be paid to the relatively small number who suffer loss. Instead of the loss being borne by one person it is shared between a larger number.

The work of an insurance company is to set up a fund by inviting a large number of people to pay small annual contributions. The company itself is not taking any risk of loss because by spreading the risk over as large a number of persons as possible, the compensation paid to subscribers who suffer loss is adequately covered by the premiums collected. Many insurance companies have built up large reserves of money which protect them against any exceptional claims that might be made upon them.

The supervision of an insurance fund is the work of officials who are called *actuaries*. An actuary's main responsibilities are the calculation of premium rates for the various types of *policies* and, in the case of a life assurance (see page 202), working out how much should be paid in bonus on 'with profits' policies.

The premium payable depends upon the nature of the risk and the amount of risk involved. The greater the risk and the greater the value of the property insured, the higher will be the premium. Thus the owner of an expensive sports car would pay higher premiums than the owner of a standard family saloon, and owners whose cars are used mainly in traffic-congested urban areas would be charged more than those who drive in rural areas where traffic is comparatively light. Similarly, in life assurance, the premium increases with the age at entry; and in fire insurance, the premium is higher where inflammable materials are used.

Uninsurable risks

There are many risks incurred in business which can be insured against. The principal risks are considered in the next section of this chapter. Some risks, however, cannot be insured, and these are termed *uninsurable risks*. They are risks which cannot be measured by past experience. Normally an insurance company works out a premium based on the number of times that an event has occurred over a past number of years. If, for example, over a long period of time, fire has destroyed business premises to the value of £500 000 a year, such premises can be insured against fire if premiums total £500 000 plus a sum to cover the insurance company's expenses and profit. Insurance can be offered only against those risks, of which the probability can be calculated. If an event is not measurable, then it is uninsurable.

Uninsurable risks must be borne by traders personally and may be guarded against only by skilful management. For example, business people must decide what goods or services to produce and in what quantities. Their knowledge of the market and their foresight must be set against the possibility that their judgement may be wrong. Business skill is shown by an ability to bear risk successfully. Between the taking of a decision to produce and the availability of the product for sale, the demand for it may change for all kinds of reasons. Fashions may change, or a 'credit squeeze' may reduce consumers' spending, so that sales of the product are not as high as anticipated. A similar risk is taken by wholesalers who hold stocks of goods. They may lose money on stock which has gone out of fashion. A third example of an uninsurable risk is the possibility that a competitor may bring out a better product at a lower price.

Despite the existence of these uninsurable risks, wise traders will arrange insurance for the maximum number of risks appropriate to their businesses. These are examined in the next section.

16.2 Kinds of Insurance

Fire

Fire insurance protects against loss through fire to buildings and their contents. If, for example, a factory is destroyed by fire the owner may rebuild with the sum of money received from the insurance company. In addition, it is possible to insure against loss of profits following a fire. Thus a serious fire which destroys premises and equipment may stop the business operating for some time. This involves a loss of profit and *consequential loss insurance* (as loss-of-profits insurance is called) provides compensation for lost revenue. Besides damage at the insured person's own premises, consequential loss insurance can also cover losses from a fire elsewhere, such as at a supplier's factory.

Burglary

Many business premises are unoccupied at night and at weekends so there is a danger of property being stolen. Burglary insurance provides cover against this kind of loss.

Fidelity guarantee

Some employees such as wages clerks or cashiers may have to handle large sums of money in the course of their work. If an employee embezzles while in a position of trust, the employer may claim from the insurance company for any sum stolen.

Motor insurance

All motor vehicles – cars, vans, lorries, etc. – must be insured *third party*. The third party is anyone who may be injured by the vehicle. The other two parties are the owner of the vehicle and the insurance company. Thus a pedestrian who has been knocked down by a firm's lorry would have a claim for compensation paid by the insurance company. In addition to third party insurance, *comprehensive cover* is available. This not only covers claims from other people, but provides compensation for loss of, or damage to, the policy-holder's own vehicle.

Plate glass insurance

Many business premises, particularly shops or showrooms, have expensive plate-glass windows and a policy may be taken out to cover the cost of replacing windows if breakage occurs.

Employer's liability

Every employer is required by law to have insurance to cover any liability against claims for injury or disease suffered by *employees at work*. In addition, cover is available for the cost of awards made to employees by *industrial tribunals*. The tribunals deal with complaints made under various laws covering such matters as equal pay, sex and racial discrimination, redundancy payments and protection of employment. The amount of compensation payable to an employer for breach of an Act may be large enough to bankrupt a small business. Hence the value of insurance to cover the cost of such an award.

Public liability

The owner of a business may become liable to pay compensation following injuries to members of the public as a result of, for example, defects in premises or the negligence of employees. Public liability insurance can be extended to cover claims arising from the sale of harmful goods. This extension is called *products liability* insurance. Examples include foodstuffs which result in food poisoning or electrical equipment which gives the buyer an electric shock.

Bad debts

All businesses selling goods on credit to other traders run the risk that some of their customers will not pay their debts. The risk can be covered by *credit insurance*. Exporters can insure against bad debts of this kind through the *Export Credits Guarantee Department (ECGD)* of the Department of Trade and Industry. The ECGD is a commercial undertaking which charges premiums according to the risk involved.

Personal accident

This form of insurance provides for payment of a lump sum in the event of death or loss of limbs or eyesight by accident, and for weekly benefits in respect of temporary total and temporary partial disablement. *Self-employed* people such as shopkeepers have, for many years, made wide use of personal accident cover. The increase in air travel, and, in travelling generally, has caused businesses to show increased interest in this form of insurance for their *employees*.

National Insurance

An employer has a legal obligation to pay a share of National Insurance for each employee. Further contributions are paid by employees and the State (from general taxation). The actual amount of the contributions and benefits from National Insurance are changed from time to time, but the main provisions are to cover *loss of earnings* through illness and unemployment. Other benefits include grants towards birth and burial expenses, pensions for widows and retirement pensions.

In one way National Insurance resembles insurance business conducted by insurance companies in that contributions are paid into a fund out of which benefits are payable. On the other hand, in addition to contributions from those entitled to draw benefit, compulsory contributions have to be paid by employers, and the State contributes from proceeds of taxation. Also, many aspects of National Insurance provide against certain eventualities, such as old age rather than against *risks*. National Insurance belongs, therefore, more to the system of social security than to insurance.

Marine and aviation insurance

All goods exported abroad will be insured against loss in transit by sea or air.

Marine and aviation insurance is undertaken by underwriters who are members of Lloyd's, and by insurance companies.

Lloyd's is an insurance market in London which deals with all kinds of risks, but is internationally famous for its work in connection with marine insurance. Although Lloyd's itself is incorporated by Act of Parliament, it does not transact insurance business as a corporation; it provides facilities for individual underwriters to do this.

The name 'Lloyd's' comes from a 17th-century coffee house in the City of London. The coffee house was owned by Edward Lloyd and much frequented by ship-owners, merchants and sea captains. At that time, marine insurance was undertaken by merchants in conjunction with their own main form of business. For the benefit of these early insurers, Lloyd displayed lists of shipping movements and from this custom has grown *Lloyd's List and Shipping Gazette,* a daily newspaper which publishes shipping news including all recorded shipping movements.

The word 'underwriter' came into use because early marine insurance policies were initialled at the bottom of the page by the various merchants who joined together to insure the larger risks. Modern underwriters still write their names under the amounts of risk they are prepared to accept.

Today Lloyd's is controlled by a committee elected by members of Lloyd's. In order to gain membership, persons have to be elected and put down substantial sums of money as security against their underwriting liabilities, The members or underwriters are not necessary specialists in insurance matters. They may, for example, be politicians or sports personalities or bankers, but all are judged to be persons of sound character and to possess considerable wealth. As underwriters they use their financial resources to insure ship-owners and merchants against losses.

The underwriters do not all meet each day, but form themselves into groups called *syndicates.* Each syndicate appoints one underwriter to accept daily business on its behalf. Underwriters who consider that they have taken too big a risk may *reinsure* some of it with other underwriters. Reinsurance prevents very heavy losses falling on any one syndicate.

All members of a syndicate have unlimited liability for their share of any loss. Lloyd's is prepared to compensate those whose claims cannot be met by the syndicate which undertook the risk.

People who wish to take out insurance are not permitted to deal directly with the underwriters. Business has to be placed through Lloyd's *brokers.* The latter are not restricted to the Lloyd's market and can, if more favourable terms are available, approach insurance companies with whom Lloyd's underwriters are in competition. However, a Lloyd's broker knows where, in the underwriting room at Lloyd's, can be found those who are likely to offer the best rates for the insurance required. Details of the insurance required are written on a *slip* and presented to an underwriter. If not satisfied with the first offer, the broker can approach other underwriters. The first underwriter to accept the risk or part of it is called the *lead*. The slip is signed and the sum covered is stated. If this sum does not cover the insurance required, the broker takes the slip to other underwriters until the full amount has been covered. In this way the risks can be spread among a number of underwriters.

In due course a policy is issued. If the insurance is underwritten by Lloyd's members, the policy will be issued by Lloyd's Policy Signing Office, which checks the slips signed by the syndicate and incorporates their individual liabilities into a single policy. Insurance companies will issue separate policies for the amount of their liability.

The broker is paid a commission by the underwriters. The amount of commission depends upon the value of the insurance.

Apart from covering ships and cargoes, marine insurance helps an exporter to obtain prompt payment for goods. When a documentary bill of exchange (see page 165) is presented to a bank for discounting, the marine insurance policy acts as *collateral security*. Without it, no bank would accept responsibility for advancing funds against the documents of title. Thus without the protection against transit risk, given by insurance, payment to exporters would have to await safe arrival of the goods.

16.3   Life Assurance

The terms *assurance* and *insurance* are of identical meaning although it is customary to distinguish between life assurance and insurance by the nature of the risk. Insurance provides cover against risks which may not happen such as fire and burglary. If no loss is suffered from fire or burglary then the insurance company will make no payment to the person insured. On the other hand, the risk covered by life assurance, namely the death of the assured person, is certain to happen. Uncertainty arises because death may occur sooner or later. In addition, the sum assured is certain to be paid either to the assured person or to a relative.

There are two main types of life assurance policy. A *whole life policy* provides a sum payable on the death of the assured person.

Premiums are paid from the date of the policy until the holder's death and people who take out this form of life assurance will never receive any money themselves. A whole life policy is suitable for those wishing to make financial provision for dependants.

An *endowment policy* provides a sum payable after an agreed number of years or at death, if this occurs before the policy matures.

This form of life assurance is a useful method of saving for a future purpose, such as a lump sum on retirement. One form of endowment assurance which may be taken out on a parent's life provides for a sum assured payable in instalments over a child's schooling period.

Usually, after two years' premiums have been paid, an endowment or whole life policy acquires a *cash surrender value*. This means a sum of money will be returned if the policy is discontinued by arrangement with the insurance company. Such a policy provides useful security for a loan from either the insurance company or a bank.

Insurance funds

Insurance funds consist of (*i*) *life* and (*ii*) *non-life* or *general funds*. The great majority of the total are life funds and these are held in trust against payments contracted to be made to policy-holders either at death or on the expiry of a specified number of years. The insurance companies are, therefore, under an obligation to invest the premiums paid to them wisely. Investments are made over the whole field of government securities, shares, property, loans and so on. Investments of life funds are long-term since much of the capital will not be required until after the policies have matured. On the other hand, general funds may need to be realised quickly in order to meet sudden large losses such as those arising from fire or disasters at sea and in the air.

A life assurance fund is rather like a reservoir, It is continuously fed by the premiums paid in by policy-holders and by the income earned from the investment of this money. Claims upon the fund arise from payments to dependants when a policy-holder dies, and from lump sum payment to policy-holders when policies mature.

If the fund is managed well, more money will gradually be collected in it than is going to be needed to meet all the claims made upon it. From time to time the value of the fund and the amount needed in the fund are calculated and the size of the surplus is worked out. In the case of a *mutual life* office (that is one in which the assets and profits belong solely to the members, i.e. the policy-holders), this surplus is distributed to the policy-holders. If the office is a *proprietary* one (that is, it is owned by shareholders) then part of the profit is paid as dividend to the shareholders and the remainder goes to the policy-holders.

Both whole life and endowment policies may be taken out on a *with profits* basis. This entitles the policy-holder, in return for a slightly higher premium, to a share of the profits earned by the insurance company. Usually 90% or more of the profits are distributed to 'with profit' policy-holders in this way.

16.4.   Taking Out a Policy and Making a Claim

The proposal form

A person who wishes to insure against a risk must fill in a *proposal form*. This is a questionnaire relating to the type of insurance being proposed. For example, a proposal form for life assurance would request details of age, height and weight, a list of illnesses, general health, the sum to be assured, etc. A person filling in a proposal form for fire insurance would have to give a description of the property, its situation, the nature of the construction, the sum to be insured, etc.

It is essential that the person completing the proposal form should do so in *utmost good faith*, that is, the proposer must make a full disclosure of all *material facts* relating to the risk. The principle of 'utmost good faith' is a basic principle of all insurance contracts. Unless the insurance company has all the information relevant to the proposal it cannot assess the risk. Examples of material facts are as follows.

For life assurance
The older a person is, the greater the risk that that person will die soon, so that if on the proposal form an age is entered several years younger than the true age, the company is being deceived into charging a lower premium.

For fire insurance
A statement that the roof of a building is made of slate whereas in fact it is thatch is a false statement causing the insurance company to assess the fire risk as less than it is.

A failure to disclose all material facts on a proposal form may cause the policy to be declared *void*, that is, the insured would have to bear the full extent of the loss.

A second basic principle of all insurance contracts is that of *insurable interest*. This means that only persons who have a direct interest in property can insure it. For example, the owner of business premises may insure that property against fire. If anyone other than the owner had the right to insure this property, there would be a temptation to arrange a fire in order to collect compensation from the insurance company. Only the owner of property benefits by its preservation or suffers through its destruction and so only the owner can insure it. In life assurance, husbands and wives have an insurable interest in each other's lives; and a creditor has an insurable interest in the life of the debtor up to the amount of the debt. If it were possible to assure the lives of other persons, the contract would be a gamble. In fact this happened in times past when people had wagers on the duration of the king's life when he went to war.

The policy

If the insurance company decides to accept the proposal made to it, the amount of premium is calculated and the proposer is sent a document called a *policy*. This provides written evidence of the contract and sets out the risk covered, the sum insured, the amount of premium to be paid and the *renewal date*.

An insurance company will send a written reminder of the renewal date of the policy several weeks beforehand. If the premium is not paid by the renewal date, then the policy *lapses* but it is the custom of insurance companies to allow *days of grace*: 15 for insurance and 30 for life assurance. The policy will be renewed providing the premium is paid before the days of grace expire.

Making a claim

When a risk that is insured against happens, the insurance company should be informed as soon as possible. The insured person will be sent a form which is used to provide the company with details of the *claim*. If the claim is relatively large, the insurance company may ask an *assessor* to inspect the damage and assess whether the sum claimed is fair and reasonable.

Compensation paid in settlement of claims is determined by the *principle of indemnity*. In no circumstances will the insured person be allowed to make a profit out of the loss. The object of the principle of indemnity is to place the insured person as far as possible in the same position as before the event happened. For example, if a house which is burned down was insured against fire for £40 000, then if the building can be reinstated at a cost of £35 000, that amount only will be paid by the insurance company. Similarly, if a car is destroyed, the insurance company will pay compensation sufficient only to replace it with a vehicle of the same make and age.

The principle of indemnity does not apply to life assurance contracts because a fixed sum is payable on the death of the assured person. Neither does the principle extend to personal accident policies: if, for example, a person loses the sight of an eye, no amount of money can restore that person to his or her state of health before the accident.

Other insurance principles relating to settlement of claims include contribution, subrogation and proximate cause.

Contribution

This is the right of an insurer who is liable under a policy to call upon other insurers, who may also be liable for the loss, to contribute to the payment. For example, if the same event is insured against under two policies, the law provides that there shall be fair distribution of the loss between the insurers concerned. Thus if a house which was insured against fire under two policies suffered fire damage, the loss would be shared by the two insurers in proportion to the amount for which the property was insured on each policy. If each policy provided equal cover, then each insurer would pay half the cost of repairs. In this way the policy-holder would be unable to make a profit out of a misfortune by claiming on both policies.

Subrogation

To subrogate means 'to take the place of'. When an insurer pays out compensation on a claim, the payment takes the place of the items damaged. For example: if, after a settlement of a claim under burglary insurance, the insurers are able to trace the stolen goods, then they are entitled to them. Similarly a car that is too badly damaged to repair (a 'write-off') becomes the property of the insurer after compensation has been paid to the owner. (The latter is not entitled to sell the wrecked car for scrap in addition to recovery compensation).

Proximate cause

The insurer need accept liability only if the loss is caused directly through the occurrence of one of the risks insured against. For example: if a person has a personal accident policy including death benefits, a claim may be made only if death results from an accident and not, for example, through disease.

Loss prevention

In order to reduce claims as much as possible, insurance companies penalise those who take little care to minimise risks and encourage those who act prudently to guard against loss. For example, in fire insurance, those who take no precautions against fire are charged higher premiums or offered limited cover, whereas premiums are reduced for those who install effective fire protection equipment. Similarly, in theft insurance, unless business-owners fit adequate locks, alarms and safes, they find it difficult to obtain cover against theft.

In motor insurance, too, insurers increase premiums above the normal rate or limit cover for people who have a bad record of accidents. Most motor insurers reduce their premiums by means of a *no claims bonus* for drivers who manage to avoid making claims over a period of years.

Another method used by insurers, which encourages insured persons to exercise prudence, and allows premiums to be reduced, is to make them pay part of their claims for damage. This is called imposing an *excess* on the policy. For instance: nearly all inexperienced drivers and drivers under 25 (statistics have shown that younger drivers are more likely to have accidents than older people, so premiums are normally higher for younger people) have an excess clause in their policies. The advantage of an excess is that it does not cost the policy-holder a higher premium, so payment is made only when an accident occurs.

16.5 Structure of the Insurance Market

The insurance market is made up of buyers, sellers and intermediaries.

Sellers

The sellers of insurance comprise insurance companies, friendly societies and Lloyd's underwriters.

Insurance companies

Insurance companies undertake the majority of insurance business. Most insurance companies are registered under the Companies Acts as joint-stock companies with limited liability.

A person who wishes to obtain insurance cover can deal with an insurance company direct. He or she may, for example, visit a branch or local office; write to a branch office or to the head office; answer an advertisement in the press; or arrange a meeting with an agent employed by the company.

The major insurance companies have branch offices in towns and cities throughout Britain.

Friendly societies

A friendly society is a special form of joint-stock company and is controlled by the Friendly Society Acts instead of by the Companies Acts. Like companies, friendly societies have to be registered and make returns to their own registrar. A friendly society is an association formed for the purpose of rendering mutual assistance to members. The societies deal almost exclusively with life and sickness assurance, using branch offices and local full-time agents.

Lloyd's underwriters

Lloyd's underwriters work at Lloyd's in the City of London and can only be contacted through Lloyd's brokers. Underwriters are personally liable for the risks that they undertake to the full limit of their personal financial resources.

Intermediaries

Insurance costs the same to buyers whether they deal direct with insurance companies or deal through a broker or agent. The broker or agent is paid by the seller of the insurance.

Brokers are agents who work independently of companies or underwriters. If they are members of the *Corporation* or the *Association of Insurance Brokers*, they are known as Incorporated or Associated Insurance Brokers. The broker's function is to advise clients and a knowledge of the market assists brokers to place the risks with the most suitable insurer. Brokers may also help policy-holders with their claims.

Lloyd's brokers are brokers who have access to Lloyd's underwriters, and all business placed with Lloyd's must pass through Lloyd's brokers. The latter also act as general brokers and they have associates and contacts throughout the world.

An *insurance agent* may be either (*a*) an employee of an insurance company or friendly society who sells only the policies of the company, or (*b*) a part-time seller of insurance in addition to carrying on a trade, profession or business. For example, solicitors, accountants, bank managers, garage proprietors, travel agents and others are often able to arrange insurance with one or a number of companies.

Buyers

Those who buy insurance include individual persons, partnerships, companies, local authorities, societies and other organisations.

London is a centre of *international insurance*. There are several hundred UK and overseas insurance companies located there, together with Lloyd's underwriters. Britain is a leading exporter of insurance services and the premium income received from abroad represents an important *invisible export*.

Test Yourself

1 How does insurance aid trade?
2 Regular payments to an insurance company are called
    _____.
3 How do the fortunate help the unfortunate in insurance?
4 What is an actuary?
5 What factors determine the premium charged?
6 Why are some risks uninsurable?
7 Give two examples of uninsurable risks.
8 Why does a trader insure against fire and loss of profits?
9 What is fidelity guarantee insurance?
10 What is (*a*) employer's liability (*b*) public liability insurance?
11 How did the word 'underwriter' come into use?
12 What is a syndicate?
13 Briefly describe how a risk is placed at Lloyd's.
14 How does marine insurance help exporters to obtain prompt payment?
15 What is credit insurance?
16 Why has there been an increase in the use of personal accident insurance by businesses?
17 Name two kinds of life assurance policy.

18 How does the risk in life assurance differ from that in insurance?
19 What is a 'with profits' policy?
20 How is a life assurance fund like a reservoir?
21 Which principles of insurance apply to (*a*) all contracts of insurance, (*b*) all contracts except life assurance and personal accident?
22 What is an insurance policy?
23 What are 'days of grace'?
24 Which principle of insurance applies to claims made on an insurance company?
25 What is 'contribution'?
26 What is 'subrogation'?
27 How do contribution and subrogation support the principle of indemnity?
28 In what ways do insurance companies try to discourage claims?
29 List the sellers in the insurance market.
30 Who are the intermediaries in the insurance market?

Chapter 17

Advertising

Most goods sold in shops are branded goods. Manufacturers give their products distinctive names or *trade marks* which are registered to prevent their use by competitors. Thus a person who goes shopping does not simply ask the retailer for a tube of toothpaste, or a packet of washing powder. Instead, their request is for Colgate or Macleans, for Persil or Ariel, or one of the other *branded* toothpastes or washing powders.

Why do manufacturers brand the goods they make with a distinctive label?

The major reason is that branding makes large-scale advertising possible. If brand names did not exist a manufacturer of margarine could increase total margarine sales by advertising, but the rise in sales might benefit competitors as well. The use of a distinctive brand name enables a manufacturer to link advertising with a particular product. A demand is created, not for margarine in general, but for a stipulated brand of margarine.

17.1 The Purpose of Advertising

Advertising is one of the *aids to trade* mentioned in Chapter 1. It assists the purchase and sale of goods in the following ways.

- *Information* is given to consumers about the availability of goods and their characteristics of colour, size, etc.
- An attempt is made to *persuade* the public to buy goods in order to increase a seller's sales and profits. An advertiser strives to create *brand loyalties* so that consumers will continue to buy a particular product in preference to that of a rival.
- If an advertising campaign is successful, the seller may pass on part of the profits in the form of *lower selling prices*. As a result, the consumer benefits, and the lower price may lead to a further increase in total sales.

It can be said, therefore, that successful advertising benefits both the consumer and the advertiser. The consumer benefits from information and possibly, lower prices; while the seller gains an increase in sales and profits.

17.2   Advertising and Marketing

The majority of firms undertake their own advertising, and in a large firm advertising will be the responsibility of the marketing division. *Marketing* is a term meaning the bringing together of sellers and buyers to complete the transactions of selling and purchasing goods. Thus a firm's marketing division is responsible for those activities concerned with the distribution of the range of products. Such activities may include:

- market research
- test marketing
- sales promotion
- advertising.

The object of *market research* is to secure information to help in formulating selling policies including the preparation of an advertising campaign. Thus the buying habits of consumers, the extent of competitors' sales, and the trend of sales over a given period of time provide important relevant facts. Market research is also used to discover why consumers purchase the goods they do; to study ways of packaging goods so as to make them attractive to the consumer; and to make sales forecasts.

Market research is conducted in several ways. Trained investigators may be sent out to *interview* wholesalers, retailers or members of the public, or *questionnaires* may be sent through the post. Government publications are studied with a view to finding estimates of future consumer purchasing power and other relevant general economic factors.

A new brand (e.g. of pet food) may be *test marketed* in a specific area of the country. The reactions of consumers in that area are studied with a view to estimating the likely national sales. At the same time, an attempt is made to assess the amount of advertising that will be necessary.

The purpose of a *sales promotion* is to create additional trade. There are two main methods: a sales event planned to boost an otherwise slack trading period; and line promotion, i.e. the selection of certain lines for special attention over a period of several months. A line promotion very often takes the form of a well-advertised reduction in retail price for a limited period.

The *advertising* media selected will be those which reach the largest number of consumers.

17.3 Methods of Advertising

Newspapers and magazines

These form the main medium for advertising.

National morning newspapers are used by advertisers (such as manufacturers) who want their advertisements to be seen by as many people as possible.

Before deciding which newspapers to use, advertisers study the number and kind of readers to whom they wish to appeal. The size of the circulation figures of different newspapers provides information as to the number of readers. Furthermore, newspapers classify their readership according to their age, sex, income and jobs. This information is very useful to advertisers.

Local papers serve a particular town or district and will be used by advertisers (such as shopkeepers) who cater for the area.

Magazines usually appeal to particular groups of people, e.g. women, or those who have a special interest or hobby such as pop music, gardening or car maintenance.

Television

Television advertising is confined to the channels controlled by the *Independent Broadcasting Authority.* No commercial advertising is permitted on BBC programmes. This method of advertising is an effective way of reaching the large number of people who comprise the viewing audience.

Advertisers can buy time on television in much the same way as they can purchase space in newspapers and magazines. Moreover, just as newspapers provide advertisers with a classification of their readers, commercial television makes available details of the number of viewers of each programme. These details are obtained from many samples of viewers' opinions which serve as a reasonable guide to what people throughout the country are watching. The information is used to calculate the size of the television audience for each programme and a 'scoreboard' of the popularity of the various serials and series programmes is produced.

Peak viewing hours are between approximately 7.30 pm and 10 pm Advertisers are required to pay higher rates during peak viewing hours than for times before or after.

Like most newspaper advertising, television advertising is aimed largely at a national audience. It will be used, for example, by manufacturers whose goods are sold throughout the country, and by retailers with nationwide branches.

Posters

Poster advertisements have one important advantage over advertisements in newspapers and on television. A newspaper is topical only for one day, while an advertising spot in a commercial break on television may last only 15, 30 or 45 seconds. Posters, on the other hand, may stay in position for many weeks and months to engage the attention of passers by.

Most posters are situated alongside main roads and in the main streets of towns. Many are directed at passing motorists who see them for only a few seconds. It follows that posters are not suitable for providing information that may take some time to read. Their chief use is to emphasise quickly and repeatedly a brand name or advertising *slogan*, e.g. 'Have a break, have a Kit Kat.'

Cinemas

The interval between films during a cinema programme is used to screen advertisements. Market research has shown that the majority of people in a typical cinema audience is composed of younger people. Consequently, advertisers wishing to appeal to young people frequently advertise on cinema screens. Thus to traders in search of new customers, the cinema is an important means of advertising.

The cinema screen is used by both local and national advertisers.

Commercial radio

Advertising for revenue is not permitted on BBC radio programmes but local commercial radio stations include advertisements in their programmes. Young people form the bulk of the listening audience and consequently much of the advertising is directed towards them.

Catalogues and leaflets

These may be pushed through the letterbox by people employed to distribute them, or they may be sent by post. Leaflets are used extensively to advertise special offers, the opening of new shops and so on. In recent years there has been a growth in the number of *advertising newspapers and magazines* which are distributed to households free of charge.

Other methods

There are many other ways of advertising, including sandwich boards, shop window and counter displays, placards on buses, on trains and in stations, packages and wrapping paper, illuminated signs, mannequin parades, and sponsorship of sporting events. Whatever means are used, advertising attempts to supply information in order to bring buyers and sellers together. The methods used by different traders will vary with the type of commodity and the kinds of people to whom the advertising is directed.

17.4   Motivations to which Advertisers Appeal

Advertisers try to persuade people that there is something particularly attractive about one brand of goods that will not be found in any of its rivals. In so doing, the advertiser appeals to certain human impulses.

Ambition

Many advertisements appeal to people's *desire to succeed* in their jobs. The successful person in the advertisement uses the product. If others who want to get on use it too (so the advertisement implies), they will also be successful. A typical advertisement of this kind features a tired business executive who is failing at work. Someone recommends a branded hot drink to be taken regularly at bedtime and before long, fortified by the deep sleep caused by the 'nightcap', the executive is successful once again.

Romance

In this type of advertisement, success with the opposite sex and the commodity advertised are connected in the consumer's mind. This is a widely used type of advertisement particularly aimed at young people. One usual form is a picture of a good-looking couple walking hand in hand by a riverside setting. The products advertised in this way include chocolates, jewellery, soap, cosmetics and perfume.

'Personality' appeal

Advertisers pay famous 'personalities', such as people prominent in sport, disc jockeys and television entertainers, to praise and recommend particular products. Consumers who admire the celebrity featured in the advertisement may be proud to drink the same beer, use the same brand of soap or eat the same food as the celebrity is supposed to do.

The desire for an easy life

Advertisers of washing-machines, vacuum-cleaners, dishwashers and other household appliances often provide a picture in their advertisements of a life made easier and simpler through the use of labour-saving devices.

Social acceptance

Advertisers of certain products often suggest that a product is desirable because without it the consumer may not be socially acceptable. A typical example is the situation where the best friend whispers that you don't get invited to play tennis or go dancing because of body odour (BO) or bad breath. However, by using the advertised brand of soap or toothpaste (so the advertisement suggests) you will soon be back with the crowd.

17.5 Consumer Safeguards

When consumers buy goods like cars, television sets and washing-machines a good deal of specialist knowledge is required in order to choose between competing brands. Very few buyers have this specialist knowledge and most rely, therefore, on the descriptions provided by manufacturers and retailers.

In order to protect consumers as much as possible from false and misleading claims for products, the *Advertising Association* publishes a *Code of Advertising Practice*. The Code sets out principles for accurate wording of advertisements and for desirable selling practices. The Code of Advertising Practice Committee is responsible for the administration of the Code. In addition, leaflets are published giving advice on the advertising treatment of various products (such as vitamins) that may have a medical association.

An independent *Advertising Standards Authority* (one-half of whose members are not connected with the advertising industry) investigates complaints from the public about advertisements.

The *Independent Broadcasting Authority* exercises control over the type and content of advertisements included in the programmes of the television and radio programme companies.

The *Trade Descriptions Act* covers advertisements. Advertising agents can be held responsible for everything said in the advertisements they produce. Consequently agencies now have a considerable responsibility to enquire into the accuracy and honesty of what goes into their advertisements.

The purpose of the Act is to ensure that, as far as possible, traders tell the truth about goods and services. Nearly everything which is said about goods which are for sale is a trade description, and a trade description must not be false.

Test Yourself

1 What is a branded article?
2 Why do the makers of goods brand their products?
3 How does advertising assist trade?
4 List the activities which may be undertaken by a firm's marketing division.
5 In what ways is market research carried out?
6 Some traders arrange their own advertising. Others ask a specialist firm called an _____ to do it for them.

7 How does advertising by a trade association differ from that of an individual firm?

8 Television advertising is confined to channels controlled by the _____.

9 What advantage (as a means of advertising) does a poster possess over newspapers and television?

10 What advantage does a newspaper or magazine have over a poster?

11 At which group of people is advertising in cinemas and on commercial radio chiefly directed?

12 List as many methods of advertising as possible that have not been already mentioned in these questions.

13 Name the main medium for advertising.

14 List some motivations to which advertisers appeal.

15 How does the Advertising Association protect consumers from misleading claims for products?

16 What is the purpose of the Advertising Standards Authority?

17 What is the purpose of the Trade Descriptions Acts?

INDEX

Index

Chambers Commercial Reference Series

COMPUTER TERMS

Sandra Carter

Computer Terms is a compact but comprehensive guide to the key computer words and phrases used in the commercial world.

- Straightforward alphabetical listing

- Helpful jargon-free explanations

- Clear simple layout for easy use

Chambers Commercial Reference Series

Straightforward guides to all the essential terms used in the business world. Ideal for students on a wide range of introductory business and vocational courses. Written in clear, simple English.

Bookkeeping and Accounting Terms
Anthony Nielsen

Business Law Terms
Stephen Foster

Business Terms
John Simpson

Computer Terms
Sandra Carter

Economics Terms
John Samuel Dodds

Marketing Terms
Martin H Manser

Office Practice Terms
Elizabeth King

Printing and Publishing Terms
Martin H Manser

Chambers Commerce Series

Bookkeeping and Accounting
David Beckwith and Harold Randall

Business Calculations
David Browning

Business Communication
Gordon Lord

Business Law
Janice Elliott Montague

Business Studies
Mark Juby

Commerce and Business
Derek Thomas

Information Technology
Hwfa Jones

Keyboarding
Derek Stananought

Marketing
Richard Watson

Office Procedures
Ruth Martindale

Reception Duties
Betty Lowe

Secretarial Duties
Penny Anson

The Business of Government
J Denis Derbyshire

Typing
June Rowley

Word Processing
Barbara Shaw

Chambers
Office
Oracle

The ideal office reference book for
managers and secretaries everywhere.
The *Oracle* gives expert and helpful
advice on all aspects of office work –
composing letters, conducting
meetings, organising conferences,
choosing equipment, planning travel;
postal services, telecommunications,
banking, advertising are covered;
there are glossaries of business,
computing, medical, legal and
financial terms *plus a full*
English dictionary.